Is It Autism, ADHD, Adolescence, or A-Hole?

Or Is It Me?

Discerning Disability from Defiance

Practical Tools for Setting Boundaries and Responding Wisely

Douglas Hodges, LMHC

This book is intended for educational and informational purposes only. It is not intended to replace individualized medical, psychological, or mental health care. The author is a licensed mental health counselor, but reading this book does not establish a therapeutic relationship. Readers should consult qualified professionals regarding specific concerns about a child's behavior or development.

The views expressed in this book are those of the author and do not necessarily reflect the views of any affiliated organizations, employers, or institutions.

Published independently by Douglas Hodges

ISBN (paperback): 979-8-9866674-3-0
ISBN (ebook): 979-8-9866674-4-7

Library of Congress Control Number: 2026905438

Cover design and illustration created with assistance of artificial intelligence tools and edited by the author.

Printed in the United States of America

For parents doing the hard work of loving and guiding
complicated kids, and for my wife and children,
who lived this journey beside me.

Contents

Introduction

Yes, you read that right. As much as I hate to admit it, my kid is sometimes an a-hole. How do I know? Because I am also sometimes an a-hole, and so are you, if you are going to be honest with yourself. If you are raising a kid on the spectrum who also has a diagnosis of ADHD, you know the struggle. Trying to discipline a disability is just plain cruel. But not encouraging boundaries and growth and blaming it all on a diagnosis is also not the answer.

To be honest, I have sat on this idea for a long time as I don't feel like I am fully succeeding in knowing the difference. My goal was to develop obvious lines that would provide a reliable path to success. But the longer I am on this journey, the more I'm convinced that there are no obvious lines. And that is the point. These A's are in a complex 4-way tug-of-war, and they all impact each other. Think of it like ingredients in a recipe. The eggs interact with the flour, sugar, and milk to make a cake. If you get the recipe right, you enjoy the cake, but if one ingredient is off, it impacts everything else.

I am convinced that the perfect recipe to make it all better does not exist, as much as I would like to give it to you (wouldn't that be nice). However, I think I can help you identify when and where the recipe is off. If the cake is dry, is it too few eggs, not enough milk, or too much flour? In the same way, if your kid's behavior/mood/decisions are off, is it autism, ADHD, adolescence, or are they just being an a-hole?

Let me say up front, there has been nothing on this planet that has been harder than raising a special needs child. Nothing and nobody else has caused me such pain, heartache, cost me as much as, frustrated me, irritated me, and just made me want to quit like raising my son with special needs. I have given up careers, relationships, and have had to mourn losses and release hopes and dreams. It is a struggle some days to stay in the battle. I have to trust that God has a purpose in all of this, and that God does not waste pain. Hebrews 11:6 (NLT) says, "Anyone who wants to come to him must believe that God exists and that he rewards those who sincerely seek him." This journey with my son has pushed me to levels of doubting God's existence and His goodness unlike anything else I have experienced. So it is with faith in the unseen that I continue to write and say: it is worth the struggle. There is a purpose in all of this. And if you are on the same journey as me, keep up the struggle. This world is not our home. Our life here is but a vapor compared to eternity. And if struggles in this life represent rewards in the next, then all who are reading this are gonna be in the fancy neighborhood in heaven!!

So here is the plan. We are going to walk through the characteristics of each "A", and describe some behaviors/thoughts/emotions that are unique to each. Then after that, the plan is to walk you through some examples of how these all can interact with each other. Hopefully, by then you will better understand the interaction, which might give you a clue about how to intervene.

The last half of this book switches the focus away from the "A's" of your person to you as the caregiver. The struggle of caring for someone with special needs has the potential to take a great deal out of you. I want to give you a few items to check on for yourself, to make sure you are as healthy as you can be. Every recipe needs an excellent chef. If the chef is off, it does not matter how good the recipe is. Self-care is one of the greatest gifts you can give your person with special needs.

Part I

Meet the A's

Before we decide how to respond to a behavior, we need to understand what may be driving it. Behaviors can look similar on the surface but may have very different sources, and the response that helps in one situation can make another worse. In this section you will meet each of the "A's" and begin learning how to tell the difference between neurological challenges, developmental changes, and behavior that still requires accountability.

Autism

Sensory and Social

While I am qualified to "wax eloquent" from a professional perspective as it relates to the symptoms of autism, instead I want to share what I have learned from the experience of living in the thick of it for almost 2 decades now. And before we get much further, the adage that "If you have met one kid with autism then you have met one kid with autism" is true. Autism is on a spectrum. This means each person has varied and different experiences with it. I cannot examine all combinations of autism. Instead, I will share from my observations both personally and professionally, as it relates to how to determine if this is the ingredient out of balance in the recipe. Autism in its basic form is processing the 5 senses differently than how those without it process their senses. By default, this has profound social implications.

Sensory

By sensory I mean the 5 senses: sight, sound, smell, touch, and taste. Any of these can be overly sensitive or under-sensitive. And what can get even more challenging is that it is not consistent. This means there are some situations where one or more of the 5 senses are stimulated and it is not an issue, but change the environment, and it is an issue. For example, kids making noise in line at a theme park, not usually a problem, but kids making noise in a Walmart, that is a problem. Same noise, but since it is in a different environment, it produces a different reaction.

Touch

Most people with autism (and this is a generality for which I am sure there are exceptions) don't like to be touched. Shaking hands or giving somebody a hug is usually a skill that has had to be learned. When you slip up and give a pat on the back or a quick hug, some may perceive it as a sort of assault or attack. Why? The part of the brain that processes the sense of touch is wired a little differently for someone on the spectrum. It is for the same reason that when you are sitting quietly on the couch and they jump on you…you perceive it as an attack, but they are just trying to connect. With the same force of touch they experienced the last time you gave them a hug to connect, they are trying to give back to you.

Sound

I swear, for certain keywords, my son has the hearing of a bat. He can be in another room, and somebody whispers the word "McDonalds" and he will pop his head out and say, "Did somebody say we were going to McDonalds?" This superpower, however, comes with some negatives. With intense hearing, he hears everything. For example; the kid 7 tables over, the dog breathing, the "eating sounds" at the table. And while I can also hear these things, my brain can filter them out as not important. I don't think his brain can as easily engage the same filter, if at all. There are certain sounds that are like fingernails on a chalkboard to him. And ironically, fingernails on a chalkboard don't create a response.

Since my childhood, I had been involved in technical productions. I have been an audio engineer for some time, and still do this on the side. It is fun for me. No matter what is going on in a mix, no matter the style of music, if my ear hears feedback, that is all

I can hear. My wife can seem to tune it out. We will be at a concert or in church, and feedback starts, and I am like a shark who smells blood; I just can't let it go, despite my wife telling me to. I get the sense that this is what it must be like for my son on the spectrum, but it is more than just feedback. It is an entire basket of sounds that is triggering. Some I know about; others I may never know about. Part of this is because he can't fully describe them to me, and another part is that I may not even be able to hear them.

Because of these potentially triggering sounds, you see a lot of kids on the spectrum with headphones. Sometimes the headphones quiet everything else down. Other times, they need music blasting in their ears to drown everything else out.

Sight

For the sense of sight to work, there has to be light. Unless you have some bat in you, you kind of need light to see. But I have found that the light itself, both the intensity of the light and the color temperature of the light, can be the thing that can produce an adverse reaction.

If the sun is shining in his eyes while we are in the car, it can create an intense reaction. Sometimes, it is the color temperature of the light. For whatever reason, the fluorescent lights in most retail stores have an impact. For some on the spectrum, it does not make a difference, but for others, the intensity of the lights and/or the color temperature of the lights can have a profound impact on one's experience.

Besides light, color can have an impact. Certain colors can set someone off. These colors could be associated with a past traumatic experience, or it could just be that a certain color is offensive or overly attractive. If you are not tracking, let me see if I can give you an example. Imagine yourself in a public space, and someone walks by in a yellow shirt. It just so happens that yellow is the trigger color.

And because this person is wearing yellow, they will get stared at the entire time. If your person is 3, this is cute. But when the person staring is 17 and the person with the yellow shirt being stared at is very attractive or has some sort of physical abnormality, it is creepy-weird (I don't know if that is a word or not, but not sure how to better describe it). The person staring couldn't care less about the appearance of the person wearing yellow; they are just laser-focused on the color yellow.

Food (Smell/Taste)

It is not just taste. Food preferences can involve temperature, texture, and smell. And previous negative experiences with a certain food can get it on the banned list. And once on that list, it is hard to get it off.

For example, French fries. Steak fries and McDonald's fries, although both pieces of potatoes that are fried in oil, are not the same thing. No amount of explaining is likely to make a difference. Coffee from Dunkin that was too hot and burned means coffee from Dunkin is on the banned list. But Starbucks is okay since it was previously served within acceptable temperature ranges.

And beyond taste, temperature, and texture, the presentation of the food is also important. If it was supposed to be on a paper plate and it got served on a ceramic plate, this may not be acceptable. It's now different and unknown. If it was last enjoyed in a bowl, but is now on a plate, it doesn't matter if it is the same food; it is now different and new, and therefore initially disliked. Dino-shaped chicken nuggets differ from star-shaped chicken nuggets, and peace be with you if you run out of the preferred one.

I have noticed that with things like hunger, there are no stages of it. Meaning, there is no "I'm a little hungry" or "I could eat". There is "not hungry", and the next notch on that scale is "I-am-about-to-die of starvation!" If somebody could give you a clue that hunger is present or growing, it would give you time to prepare. And when you are preparing food, actively cooking, and turn around and see snacks being grabbed, it is easy to get frustrated. Because autism impacts how sensations like hunger are experienced, when it hits, the hunger is now, not in 10 minutes when food is ready. Even if it is a pre-approved food that you are cooking from scratch, the hunger felt now is intense!

Food also carries with it several smells. Smells of the individual ingredients, smells of the cooking process, and maybe even the smells of the person laboring to prepare it all! Some of those smells bring joy and excitement; others are repulsive. In food preparation, if you are making a preferred food like a grilled cheese (assuming this is a preferred food), but some of the cheese oozes out and burns on the pan, that is a particular smell that may ruin the experience of the preferred food, and could place it on the banned food list.

Driving a car through smells can also be a challenge. Even if only brief, a smell can trigger an intense reaction. Some examples might be a sewage truck passing by, a skunk on the side of the road, somebody driving by thinking it is April 20th every day…whatever the smell might be, it can be experienced intensely by someone with autism.

Parts vs. Whole

I have seen parts of certain movies, and heard the pre-chorus to a certain set of songs thousands of times. For some reason, the parts are more important than the whole. Songs I used to love I now avoid, as the playing of that song will trigger a need to hear one phrase over, and over, and over (did I say over) again. My wife and I often joke that he has career potential as a black ops interrogator for the CIA!

I secretly picture a hardened criminal sitting down at a metal table in a concrete room. The normal interrogator gets in his face and yells, "Tell me where they are!". The criminal laughs, knowing he will never break. Then the door opens, and my son walks in with his music playing on his phone, and beads of sweat suddenly appear on the forehead of the criminal, and he begs… "I'll tell you whatever you want to know, I swear… it was my mom, she is the boss! Just get him out of here!!!"

But those parts of the whole are soothing. Having the ability to control the flow of the song or movie has a bit of a rush to it. Legos and puzzles are connected to this. Being able to take things apart, and put them, or portions of them, back together scratches an itch in an autistic brain.

Stimming

Speaking of scratching that itch, I think now is a good time to talk about stimming. This is where many people who are not that familiar with autism tend to first notice something. For some, this involves hand movements or foot movements. For my son, it's dancing. No, not Fred Astaire style dancing, but a series of bodily movements that usually involved moving in a circle, jumping, spinning, and all of this while usually listening to some sort of music. And it is very much so not on beat. It is almost hard to imitate it being this offbeat. Most people usually fall in line with some sort of rhythm, but not him. He has his own beat.

When he was about 7 or 8, we were at Disney Springs. My wife went to get a coffee, and the boys and I were outside waiting. There was a break dancer and a DJ in this area who were performing. Something about the music just struck a nerve. And my son started to "dance" because he was likely overstimulated from a day at Disney, and just needed to get it all out. So, I just let him. The dancer was initially glad to have some crowd participation, so he tried to dance with him, but was just not able to keep up. Remember, there is no pattern and no rhythm to it. But somehow the DJ was able to find a beat that worked. The dancer, not so much. After trying to be his wingman, the dancer just kinda backed off. At about this time, I looked up, and a crowd was forming. People thought he was part of the show. I texted my wife to come outside, and she walked out to a crowd of people who were watching with anticipation our son stimming. And then, mid-song, he decided he was done and just stopped and walked off. Picture Forest Gump on the road after running thousands of miles, just stopping and saying, "I think I'll go home now." The crowd was like, "What just happened" and the dancer was like, "What just happened" but we knew. He was overwhelmed with all that was going on, and needed to work it out. He did, and did not care where he was or who was watching, and he got it out and was now done. We had him thank the dancer and DJ, trying to model a social skill, and then we departed.

Social

When your senses are over (or sometimes under) stimulated, social interactions are even more challenging. So many of our social interactions are based on noticing and interpreting social cues from others. And there is so much nuance that it is hard even for a neurotypical to know the difference between a "flirty" wink versus an "I-have-an-eyelash-in-my-eye" wink.

For many on the spectrum, the lack of subtly is on full display with social interactions. It's hard enough to communicate, so when you do, why not tell somebody exactly what is on your mind? For a long time, and it may still be partially true, I questioned whether my son had an internal monologue. Meaning, I'm not sure he ever thought about saying something that he did not say. In some ways, there is an authenticity to this that is admirable and respectable. And for those in relationships with people on the spectrum, this honesty, as brutal as it might be, can be a strength. But I know for me, if I said everything I thought, I'd be in jail or dead!!

So in social situations, when there is already a challenge to understanding social cues based on sensory distortions, responding to the back and forth of a normal conversation leaves most people on the spectrum out. We talked about one of these already in our section on touch. A pat on the back, intended to be a congratulatory interaction, because of autism can easily be interpreted as a physical attack. "I thought he was my friend. Why is he hitting me?" The wink that intends to say, "Hey cutie, I'd like to get to know you," can easily look like, "You wanna get in my panel van and get human trafficked?"

Now might be a good time to talk about sarcasm. For many on the spectrum, it does not exist. If you have not taken the time to see how much of your life involves sarcasm, just spend a day observing how many times you say something you don't mean, or hear something that was intended to be interpreted opposite of how it was said. Let me see if I can give you some examples.

"Dad, can you take me to the store?"

"Sure, let me just stop everything I'm doing so that you can get whatever you want!"

Intention: you are being selfish and not letting me take a nap, and I'm not taking you to the store.

Interpretation: Dad is going to take me to the store

Friend: "Wow, look at that outfit!"

Intention: that turtleneck you are wearing in July, in Florida, in 95° heat, looks stupid.

Interpretation: my outfit looks good and people like it.

Parent: "Looks like you got a lot accomplished today." (As he sits in a room covered in clutter.)

Intention: you are lazy and did nothing all day

Interpretation: thank you for noticing. I had to go through all these boxes to find the toy I was missing.

I have also found that many kind and well-intentioned people have made situations worse by not giving a straightforward answer. Because people fear hurting the feelings of others, particularly those with special needs, they give answers like "maybe", "we'll see", or "not yet", which are all interpreted as "yes". And it creates more problems when the person continues to press for whatever you "agreed" to, which creates divides in relationships as you thought you said no, when in fact you said maybe, and while most would have heard no, someone on the spectrum heard yes.

Saying things like, "No, I will not give you my number, but I'm happy to hang out with you and talk to you at this event" is really hard for others to say as it sounds harsh, but is very much so what is needed. It clearly answers the question and sets the boundaries. While it sounds harsh, it is not interpreted as such. It is a message that can be clearly received.

Restaurant

Let me introduce a common event that we will keep going back to in each section to illustrate how each of these ingredients are at play. A common thing that has been a real challenge for me is going to a restaurant. Not like a fancy Micheline Star restaurant, I'm talking anything from McDonald's to Olive Garden. My son categorizes restaurants as either pay-to-eat or pay-to-leave restaurants. Some days, we only have emotional resources for a pay-to-eat, and on others, we roll the dice on a pay-to-leave place.

Restaurants can be very sensory-stimulating places. There are the smells of food, the sounds of people, plates, background music, the temperature of the room and the food, just to name a few. And whether this is a new versus a familiar space is also a factor. If the space, the procedures to get food, the layout of the tables, and the food choices are the same as last time and last time was a good experience, this lessens the variable. But there are always people and sounds that can be different. With autism, these sensory experiences — any of these experiences — can be overwhelming. But when you add all of them together into the equation, this makes going out to restaurants a challenge.

Since communication elements are a feature of autism, it makes it hard to verify what I am about to say, as he just can't communicate this to me. But as an outsider looking in, I have gathered that these sensory elements are just not fully understood as annoying. As such, it makes it hard for him to communicate what is going on. For example, it would be wonderful if my son could say, "Dad, I want to have an enjoyable experience at this restaurant, but the kid talking 7 tables over is really annoying me because of the high pitch of his voice. Do you think we could sit somewhere else?" Instead, he is just fully set off, and there is nothing (as far as I can tell based on my experience) that is causing this as I am not even registering there is even a kid 7 tables over or that he is making noise. For those on the spectrum, I imagine it is like me being expected to explain that water is wet or that concrete is hard. It is just such a basic part of life, so why go through the extra effort to communicate this to somebody?

To address this, we have learned to pay attention to other bodily cues that might give us some insight that he is getting overwhelmed. There are some obvious signs like stimming behaviors, but smaller things like the size of his pupils give us some insights that something is happening, even if he can't tell us.

Summary of the Autism Ingredient

- senses over or under stimulated

- Routines vs flexibility

- Social struggles

- Difficulties communicating.

ADHD

As a mental health counselor, one question I would most get from parents regarding ADHD was, "If he has an attention DEFICIT disorder, how can he play video games for 14 hours straight and not even use the bathroom? If he can do that, he can pay attention in other areas like math class!!??"

Stimulation

Attention Deficit Hyperactivity Disorder (ADHD) by itself is difficult to understand, both for those who have it and for those who live with someone who has it. We could spend a lot of time discussing professional diagnostic language, but let's see if I can describe this differently. Have you ever been on a boat or a jet ski? You can't turn a jet ski that is not moving. The faster it is going, the easier it is to turn. And a boat has to hit a certain speed in order to work at maximum efficiency. ADHD is similar. There is a certain amount of stimulation that has to happen for the brain to get fully engaged. So things like video games, which fully engage the brain, allow those with ADHD to function maximally and focus fully. Video games can place those with ADHD in their sweet spot, and they can stay in that zone for hours. But when the brain is not fully engaged, like in math class, they will do things to engage their brains, and those things are not always helpful. Things like talking, telling jokes, putting gum in the person's hair in front of them, you name it. Anything to get some additional stimulation.

Hyper Focus

A factor in stimulation is desire and enjoyment. The more you want to do something and the more you enjoy it, the easier it is to stay focused on it. While this is similar for anybody, for those with ADHD, it is on a whole different level. This is where we can get into the concept of hyperfocus. This was the question at the beginning of this chapter.

When you are excited about a task, or the task is optimally stimulating, you can lock in and just do it. This can feel like a superpower or even a high for those with ADHD.

Some have even learned how to induce this by adding extra stress into their lives. By waiting until the last minute, or by having a big enough reward/consequence, you create an environment where the stakes are high enough that you force yourself into hyperfocus. Why work on an extensive project an hour a night, when the night before the stress of having to have it all done tomorrow will engage hyperfocus and you can stay up all night and knock it out? Why keep your room clean when you can put it off for weeks and, under fear of a punishment or loss of a privilege, can set everything else aside and clean the whole thing all night? And for about 10 minutes, you have a clean and organized living space!

You don't notice the damage this does to your health or relationships because you pulled it off. You completed the task. And to be honest, our culture celebrates production way more than we do the process to get the product, so you get rewarded with the grade or the contract, or whatever the reward is.

Distractions

But ADHD is not all about seasons of hyperfocus. On the regular, it is way too easy to get distracted. If you are not fully engaged in a task, and particularly a task that you don't enjoy, anything, and I do mean ANYTHING, can draw your attention away. "Hey look, a squirrel!" Is a real thing with ADHD. It can be an external stimulus or some random though that you just roll with in your brain...*if the color blue had a relationship with the number 5, what would their babies look like*...and before long the bell has rung and you are still on number 5 of the 20 question test you are now going to fail, that you stayed up all night to study for!

Food

Impulse control is a feature of ADHD. When you want something, you want it now. Delayed gratification and ADHD don't get along. So, food cravings are a big deal with ADHD. And if stimulant medications, which are a category of meds frequently prescribed to help with ADHD, are being taken, this can really mess with one's appetite. Stimulants have a side effect of being appetite suppressants, so if one is on a stimulant for ADHD, they will not be hungry while that medication is in their system. But as soon as the medication wears off, the person taking it will be starving and will eat the paint off the walls if that is all that is available.

Foods can also have a negative impact on ADHD, such that some foods can exacerbate the symptoms. Typically, sugar and ADHD don't get along, but sugar is a great quick-fix and is usually a craving! Foods that can be ready quickly are almost always preferable to healthier foods that take time to prepare. And the quicker the food option is, the less likely it is to be healthy.

Restaurant

So let's revisit our example of going to a restaurant to see what role ADHD might be playing. First, and this is bigger than we would like to admit, does your person want to be at that restaurant? If the answer is yes, then there is a high likelihood that ADHD will not be as big of a factor. If they do not want to be there, anything can be a distraction. All the same sensory elements are still happening, and this can make it difficult to look at a menu and decide. If there is any wait or delay, ADHD will have difficulty with this. This can open up the possibility of annoying others, ripping up napkins, getting up and down, frequent restroom trips, or just doing anything to get an adrenaline spike to make the experience more exciting.

Then, when the food arrives, they probably don't like what they ordered (or worse, what someone ordered for them because they would not decide) because they did not want to be there and ignored the menu. They will probably only pick at the food or steal from another person's plate because it looks better, or just to annoy someone else and get a thrill.

And let's not overlook that there is a loudness about all of this with ADHD. None of what I have just described will happen at an acceptable volume for a public space.

And if stimulant medication is in the mix for your person, there is a very good chance they are not hungry, or are between doses and are starving. And the lack of food not coming fast enough is also an issue.

And when you finally lose it and go off on them, the meal is done, and you complete the walk of shame to the car, apologizing to everybody along the way, they tell you on the ride home it was a fun dinner and we should do that again. Why? Because you losing your feces was fun and stimulating, and they want to do it again.

Adolescence

Prior to the 1900s, the term "adolescence" was not really a thing. Most cultures around the world celebrated the passage from child to adult around the ages of 12-13. A Bar or Bat Mitzvah happens at 12-13; confirmation in Catholicism historically was around the age of 11-12, but now can be anywhere from 7 to 16. Starting at age 12, if you were a Masai boy, you could start your hunt for a lion to prove you were a man. I am not suggesting that 12-year-olds should have adult rights; I am only trying to show that we used to give adult responsibilities to those we now consider adolescents.

We know now that one's brain does not fully develop into an adult brain until around 26. This does not mean you are a child until you are 26, but that your brain has not fully engaged its adult capacities. It has been interesting to track the age at which children begin puberty over the years. Prior to 1900, the average age that puberty started was 16. By 1950, it was 13-15. Today, the average is 12. That's an average, meaning some can start puberty around the age of 8. That can be second grade for some people!

So here is the point. Historically, you had adult privileges and responsibilities sometimes years before you had gone through puberty. Now, you experience puberty earlier than anyone in history has ever recorded, yet people treat you like a child for almost a decade after your body physically matures.

This has created a unique set of tensions and contradictions we now call adolescence. You want to be an adult, your body is like that of an adult, but your mind often (or at random) acts like a child.

At one point in my life, I worked closely with college-age single adults, people ages 18-24. Occasionally, some people were absolutely convinced they were in love with their soulmate and had to marry at 18 to spend their life with that person. They would complain to me about their parents not being supportive of their life plan. They would cite as evidence to support their plan that their grandparents (who had been married for 60 years) got married when they were like 16-17 years old. With as much kindness and love as I could muster, I would then remind them that at 17, their grandfathers had 2 full-time jobs and his own home that was almost paid off! All they had was a high score on Call of Duty (the popular game then). 17 in 1950 was not the same as 17 in the 2000s.

I am not looking to go into the reasons for all of this. There are other works that go into these details if you are interested. I only want to point it out because this is a tension point of adolescence. You want adult freedoms with childlike responsibilities. Your body is ready to be an adult, but your mind is not.

Hormones

The role that hormones play in adolescence cannot be overstated. While we won't break out a biology textbook, things like testosterone (for guys), estrogen (for gals), adrenaline and growth hormones are legitimately changing an adolescent. A rush of testosterone can trigger aggression. Adrenaline gives you the energy to fight or flee. But when it is running system tests in adolescence, random firings can make one want to just be loud or run. And conversely, when you like how that feels, you might start chasing things that can naturally trigger it. So you just pick a fight or engage in some other stupidly dangerous behavior to flood your body with adrenaline. It is interesting to note that men who are suffering from undiagnosed and untreated clinical depression may just go chase an adrenaline rush with very dangerous activities like auto racing, skydiving, bull riding, etc. Where do you think they learned that an adrenaline rush feels good? Adolescence.

It is for this reason that an adolescent can just pick a fight. For absolutely no reason, in a perfectly peaceful moment, they pick at people. In my house, we call that poking the bear. Why? Running from a bear trying to attack you has a certain rush to it.

Limbic System

This is the part of the brain that helps regulate your emotions and soothe you. It is also where our brains process pleasure and rewards. At its core, the limbic system keeps us alive by helping us respond to attacks or threats. And if you have not seen where this is going yet, during adolescence it is also developing. On some days it is overactive and on other days not so much.

It is for this reason that adolescents can be emotionally reactive to the smallest of stimuli, and the next moment be looking for really intense behaviors to get a sensation. Some have resorted to cutting or self-mutilation to force a response out of the limbic system, as the pain of a blade is the only way they can feel something or release something. Tattoos, in what I'm sure will be an unpopular opinion by many, can be an extension of this for adults. It hurts, but as soon as you are done, you want another one because the pain of the tattoo stimulates the limbic system to generate a response to soothe you.

As adolescents are growing and developing, this portion of their brain (and by the way, this is not the only part of the brain that is developing) can trigger neurotransmitters at the drop of a hat, with hormones running wild and crazy. No wonder emotions and decision making are out of whack. Please hear me; this does not excuse inappropriate behavior or poor decisions, but it helps make it understandable. This is also good to know when it comes time to discipline an adolescent. Some of what they are doing, they may just not have control over. But other times they do. To blame every poor decision in adolescence on brain development is not wise, but to ignore its impact is also ill-advised.

Physical Changes

While we have talked about changes in the brain, there are also changes in the body. Not just the changes in development of sexual organs we already mentioned, but the body itself is changing. I have heard it described in terms of a vehicle. Childhood is like driving a sports car, and adolescence is like driving a school bus. Feet, legs, arms and hands are getting bigger and an astonishing rate, and you are just not used to them yet. So, you run into things, drop things, make messes, get injured, etc.

You also need more sleep. But as we will discuss in a bit, that can be a challenge. You also don't want to be told what to do. And having bedtimes is for babies, and you are almost an adult! You should get to decide when you go to bed and when you get up.

Food

These changes require fuel. For some, that can look like eating anything and everything in sight. But this is not the case for all. Food preferences can lead to pickiness, and sometimes an overindulgence in foods that usually are not that healthy. But hey, your body is young and your metabolism is strong, so no harm/no foul until adulthood when those poor eating habits catch up to you.

Food can take on different meanings because of social pressures to look (or not look) a certain way; denying one's body of legitimate needs can also be in play to accomplish these goals. Just one of the many tensions in adolescence. You need to eat and are hungry, but you don't want to be fat, or you don't want to spill anything on yourself, so you don't eat at the table/restaurant around others. Then later, when all alone, you pound an entire bag of chips or Oreos to stave off hunger, but are unintentionally contributing to the very thing you had hoped to avoid!

Social Changes

It is hard to overstate the importance that friends have on an adolescence. And for most reading this, you went through adolescence without social media. Today, when others could record and comment on every moment of your life, this exponentially increases the importance that social standing and concerns of others has on adolescents. Compared to your adolescent experience of crossing the Grand Canyon on a donkey, theirs is like jumping it with a motorcycle Evil Knievel style! (Or Duke Kaboom if you are not that old;-))

There is this great tension to be your own person, separate and unique, but also to fit in. This plays out in choices related to food, fashion, physique, music, entertainment, religion and politics. And these days, you must have an opinion on everything, and failing to condemn someone else's poor behavior seems to be equivalent to supporting the poor decision! The pressure to keep up with it all can be overwhelming and exhausting. Especially when your body is tired, hungry, changing, coursing with new hormones, and your brain can't decide if it is an adult or a child most days.

I Don't Know

Early in my career, I sat in counseling sessions with adolescents for 30 minutes, asking every question under the sun to get engagement. And every response was the same: "I don't know". This is the go-to phrase of adolescence. It can mean a lot of things. I'll list a few.

- This is stupid

- You are stupid

- I'm tired

- I'm hungry

- I don't trust you

- You don't really care about me

- I don't want to be here

- I've never thought about it

- I don't want to think about it

- I've thought about it, and I really do not know

- Is it time to go yet?

- I don't want to say

- There is no way to make you understand

Later in my career, after a parent went to the waiting room, I would ask the adolescent if they wanted to be there. If they did, and many did, they would engage. Others would tell me, "No. They are forcing me to come." I would ask if they wanted to talk, and they would tell me no, so I would go to my desk and read a book or catch up on notes. After 15-20 minutes of silence, they would ask if I really was not going to say anything. And I would basically tell them I respect their space, and I will not force them to talk. Their parents are likely going to make them continue to come, so if they wanted to work on homework, read a book, take a nap, etc., it was up to them. Some would start talking then as they had their boundaries respected. Some would continue in silence and would come in the next session ready to talk. But when the "I don't know's" would start, I'd hand them a chart with a similar list on it and ask them which "I don't know" they were using. This let me know how to break the ice and overcome the barrier.

Restaurant

Going to a restaurant as an adolescent has a lot to do with who is there. If friends are with the adolescent, they can have a great time. But if forced to endure the inhumane torture of having to go to a restaurant with your parents, with the possibility of being spotted by others who might take a pic and post about you having a loving family…the horror! And we have not even talked about the possibility of an embarrassing sibling being present!

Because of changes in the body, food preferences can be constantly changing. What you enjoyed last time might taste different now, so you might not want what you ordered. If you are at a pay to leave restaurant, you probably fill up on the tasty bread they brought out and cannot eat the actual entrée you ordered.

But throughout this experience, your adolescent will probably be (or want to be) on their phone. We will talk more about this later, but their phone is like a part of them. Telling them not to use their phone is like asking them not to use their elbows! Besides, it's much more enjoyable to talk to their friends who understand them than to say, "I don't know," to their parents repeatedly.

Is it Autism, DHD, Adolescence, or A-hole?

A-hole

I saved this ingredient for last, mainly because I just don't want to assume this first before ruling out all the others. I would like to think that I have invested in my kid in such a way that I have not trained someone to be an a-hole, and that I have good parenting skills and have modeled good life decisions. But if we are going to be honest, we are all a-holes from time to time, so he may just be modeling what he is seeing.

By a-hole, I basically mean one's sin nature. This is the concept of "I want what I want, and I don't care how it impacts others." Oh, and, "I want it now, ideally prior to now."

While this is very similar to adolescence, where I draw the line is when you know what the right answer is, the right thing to do, and you on purpose choose something else. Sometimes you are choosing this because you don't want to take the time to go through the right channels to achieve your result the right way. Other times, the wrong way just seems more fun. This differs from adolescence, where behavior is more influenced by hormones. This is a choice. Typically, a choice to choose self over anything else. Let's see how this might play out in a few areas.

Complaining

While all who compline are not a-holes, complaining is the on-ramp to a-hole city. Complaining is not equal to a-hole, but it pushes the needle in that direction. When you complain, you are basically saying you are not getting your way. People, things, systems, are not going the way you want them to go. Where you cross the line into the land of a-holery has to do with what comes after the complaint. If you look at your situation and figure out how you might be the problem, and then fix yourself, congratulations, you are exercising healthy maturity. If you evaluate what you have control over and use the resources and influence you have to make the situation better; not an a-hole. Maybe you recognize you lack the ability to control this situation, and assertively address the concern with the proper authority. If so, you are not an a-hole but a leader.

But if you start down the complaining path, and you blame others, gossip to others about it, try to take control over what is outside of your legitimate control, or just take what you want…you've got it…a-hole. How does this play out?

Parent: "I need you to clean up your room."

But you don't want to clean up your room. You want to play your games. It is no fun cleaning up your room. Instead of recognizing that someone provided you with a free place to live and sleep, and gave you enough things so you have more than you need and can even dirty a room, a few a-hole responses might be…

I will not, and you can't make me.

Nobody else in this house has to clean their rooms, so I don't see why I have to.

It's as clean as it needs to be. It's my room, and I am not bothered by it.

Sure, in a minute. (with no intention of ever doing it)

" " (you read that right, no response)

Picking up one thing… "I picked it up, so it's clean."

Slam the door to prove your point that you don't want to do it.

A few non-a-hole responses might be:

"I appreciate the discipline and structure you are providing me, and I am certain it will reap benefits in my future. Even though it is not my natural inclination to clean my room, I acknowledge this is your home that you pay for, and I will do my part to maintain order in the portion you have graciously allowed me to dwell in." (Okay, if one of my kids said that to me, I would know they were being an a-hole by saying it sarcastically; nevertheless, it would be nice to hear.)

"Yes, sir."

"I have just started a new level in my game. Would it be okay if I began this in about 8 minutes when I have completed this level?"

"Sure, by when would you like me to have this completed?"

"I am feeling a little overwhelmed with all that is going on in my room; could you provide me with some guidance on where to get started first?"

"There are things in my room that do not belong to me, and I am not sure what to do with them. Could you help me figure out what to do with the stuff that others have placed in my room?"

Adolescent: "Nobody is doing their job in this group project!"

On a personal note, I hated group projects in school. Even in the workforce, I am not a fan of group projects. Unless you are in an environment with passionate and motivated professionals, group projects deteriorate to one smart and driven person getting taken advantage of by smart, lazy people who eventually become CEO's of companies and get paid 10-100 times more than the smart and driven people who make them successful. But I get that part of the education experience is learning to work with others, and learning to work together, as this is a big part of most workforces. So when you are on a group project and it is not going well…

A-hole responses:

> "I am going to tell the teacher that nobody else helped on this so they all get poor grades."

> Start a group chat and exclude the people not working and tell everybody else how lazy the non-workers are.

> "We've got a smart kid in our group. He/she will just do it, and I will take the credit, so I will just continue to do nothing."

> "I'll just do it all and forget about everybody else."

Non-A-Hole Responses

> Schedule a meeting with the other group members and discuss responsibilities.

> Complete the portion assigned to you, and share with the other group members and ask for feedback.

> Agree to help others with their parts, ensuring you are not doing their work for them.

> Identify any challenges that the group may face and work out a plan to overcome those challenges.

Do it all yourself and blow it out of the water, and brag at the presentation about how helpful your group has been with this (ok, so that one is a passive a-hole, not that I have ever done that:-))

Desires

A-holes are ultimately slaves to their own desires. When they want something, they have to have it. If they are hungry, they will take food that is not theirs or complain to hasten getting their hunger satisfied. Upon seeing an object they want, they will demand it be secured for them now, or else they will just take it. If they are lonely and want company, they will invade your space to get connection, whether you want to give it or whether or not you are awake.

Connected to their desires are timing and effort. There are better ways to accomplish their end goal, but that usually involves time and effort. What typically earns you an a-hole badge is when you want somebody else to do the work for you, and you want that work done now. A second aspect is a complete lack of empathy of how your requests impact others.

Think about some of the a-hole bosses you have had. They show up 15 minutes before it is time to leave for the weekend and assign you a 2-hour project they need immediately that they could just as easily do themselves, but they have to go meet their spouse for dinner. So they assign it to you. There is no thought of how this impacts you and your family, and no "thank you" when you stop everything to deliver it. The difference between this and your kid being an a-hole is that you can resign from your job. But with your kid…apparently there is a limit to the age you can drop them off at a fire station in a washing machine box…I mean, or so they tell me :-)!

But I should also note, a-holes get results. There is a reason so many get promoted in companies. They get the job done. A-holes can make others complete tasks, but leave a wake of destruction in their paths.

Pride

Believing they are more important than others runs deep with the a-hole. Think about most infants you have been around. They want what they want when they want it. They cry, and most of the time we give them what they want. This goes on for a long time in early development. They can't even talk, and yet our world revolves around them. And it should. They are needy and utterly helpless. But when they become capable and still exhibit the same behaviors, thinking they are better than the rest of us or too good to do the work themselves, this is where a-holes form.

And if we as parents are being honest here, we kinda have a hand in this. Sometimes it is just easier to do things for them rather than have an argument. So you just empty the dishwasher, fold the laundry, clean the room, pick up the toys…rather than make them do it for themselves. Sure, you tell yourself you could win the argument and make them do it, but you are just too tired to have the argument. Please hear me. I'm not judging; I'm confessing. I get it. The struggle is real. It may be necessary to sacrifice long-term good for momentary peace. Remember, we are a-holes too sometimes!! It can just be easier to take care of it yourself, which leads to our next point.

Lack of Consequences

If your little precious never has to face the consequences of their actions because you or others always bail them out, their response is usually not appreciation, but a-hole. They learn to expect it. So much so that there is no deterrent to engaging in such behavior.

In scripture, the apostle Paul encountered this line of thinking in his letter to the believers in the city of Rome. He spent a lot of time teaching about this amazing concept that was (and is) not really present in world religions and is unique to Christianity: grace. In a nutshell, and to the embarrassment of my theology professors, I'll give you a quick overview. You do stupid stuff, and God gives you gifts. It's "amazing grace" when you are the wretch getting saved, but it is infuriating grace when you are the victim and your perpetrator gets a bonus. The people of Rome, who were clearly a-holes by our definition, decided that if they did more stupid stuff, they could keep getting more grace. So Paul confronts them in Romans 6 when he sarcastically asks if they should continue in sin so that grace may abound. Then he gives them a written beating because their thinking was so stupid.

But we all, and especially our kids, do the same thing. We both take advantage of the grace we receive. And receiving grace is great. We desperately need it. But how we react to it leads to our next point.

Ungratefulness

When you have limited or no appreciation for others or things in your life, your a-hole nature is fully displayed. While this is connected to lacking empathy, being ungrateful goes much deeper. Empathy takes the time to see how others are impacted or feel, whereas ungratefulness is more about self and how you feel. Regardless of what others provide, you believe it is basic and necessary.

Ungratefulness is like fertilizer to all these a-hole seeds we have been discussing. You are not happy with what you have…so you complain. You are not satisfied with what you have…so you become a slave to your desires that take you further than you want to go, cost you more than you wanted to pay, and keep you longer than you wanted to stay. And you don't care how many people you hurt along the way to getting what you want. When you are ungrateful, you don't care about the consequences of your actions, and are often not even aware that others have prevented you from destruction. You think you deserve their sacrifices and that they are not sacrificing enough for you because you are better than they are.

Restaurant

With this ingredient, I can share a story from my childhood. While on a family vacation we could barely afford, our family stopped for dinner at a restaurant. I believe the choice was Cracker Barrel or something similar. Four out of the five of us agreed to this restaurant. My brother, however, objected. I really don't know or remember why he objected, just that he did not want to go there. So he stated he would just sit in the car and not eat. My father was having no part of this and demanded that he go in and enjoy the meal that was being provided for him. I believe my father used the term "ingrate" to describe the behavior. My dad frequently charged him with being an ingrate, so it's hard to recall if he used the term here, but it would be surprising if he didn't, considering how often he used it.

Now, before I continue, I feel like I should set the scene on the financial status of our family. In my family growing up, we could not order cheeseburgers at fast-food restaurants, because the cheese was like $0.20-0.30 extra, and we had cheese at home and could put cheese on our burgers there if we wanted cheese.

So back to the roadside Cracker Barrel. After being forced against his will to enter the restaurant, we eventually got to our table. As my mom was diligently figuring out how to most economically order so the family of five could all eat with the least amount of money being spent, my brother picked up a menu. The waitress comes by, and my mom orders. Right as the waitress records the family order and is about to walk away, my brother peeks out from over his menu, and orders the most expensive thing on the menu. Not because he particularly liked the most expensive item on the menu; I'm not even certain he knew what it was. To save face, my dad, through clenched teeth, tells him he better eat all of it or face the consequences. (It was the 80s, so he was not gonna lose his phone!)

After a tense wait, our food arrived. While four of us divided what my mom ordered, a feast fit for a king, a very fat king, was presented to my brother, who proceeded to eat every last bite. He may have even licked the plate to prove a point.

This was pure a-hole. While he was an adolescent, this was not influencing his decision making or behavior. He knew what he was doing and did it with a certain pride and flair. There was no gratitude expressed for the meal. He was proving his point. I will get what I want, and will punish anybody in my way.

Part II

Interaction Examples

Knowing the definitions of each of our A's is important, but the real challenge is understanding how they interact with each other. The goal of writing this is to help parents and guardians better understand what is influencing the behavior and choices of their person, so when trying to correct this behavior you have a better idea of what tools to use. By understanding what is causing the behavior, particularly the behaviors you don't want, the idea is you will have a much easier time of addressing the issue at the root. The problem is that it is never clearly in one specific category, because all 4 A's interact with each other and are present all the time. While we have been talking through the experience of going to a restaurant, I want to describe examples of how everyday life is impacted by our four A's. By seeing this play out in common lived experiences, I hope it will further clarify the subtle dance that can take place. We will structure the experiences around the idea of "A Day in the Life" of someone with some of these struggles. We will start in the morning and end the day with bedtime routines. Along the way, we will hit topics like getting ready to leave, school, finances, and phones. We will take you through each of these experiences with each A in mind, and show how some actions and reactions may be similar, but are sourced in a different A. Some of these reactions may clearly be in one category, but most will fox-trot from one to the other with no rhyme or meter. You will polka your way into a tango and Paso right into your Doble. Confusing? That may have been intentional. Strap on your boots/shoes/sandals/socks for the wildest dance party you never wanted to attend!

Morning Routines

Mornings happen every day. Every day, at some point, it is necessary to get out of bed and get ready for the day. Every day. Either consciously or unconsciously, a set of routines are developed around this. And if those are healthy routines, it sets the day up for success. And even if good routines are planned, whether self-planned or planned by others, autism, ADHD, adolescence, or being an a-hole can very much so influence or hijack a morning routine and, by extension, the rest of the day.

Autism

Routines and autism are like butter in southern cooking. Routines are in everything with autism. And when properly applied, these routines can be very helpful. They can help you get up at a certain time, eat the same thing for breakfast you have eaten for the last 5 years, put on clothes, brush your teeth, or comb hair. All of this can be really healthy, and if you are in this type of situation, I want to encourage it. But I want to point out two areas where challenges can exist.

First, when you are forced to go off routine for circumstances beyond your control, mornings can get a lot more complicated. For the things out of your control, I am talking about things like the toothpaste running out, the power going off, the company that makes the microwave breakfast sandwich goes out of business, preferred clothes are not clean (likely because they were worn yesterday). Maybe it's a teacher workday on a random Tuesday so you don't need to catch a bus or you or somebody integral to the routine is sick. I can only imagine you are now recounting some traumatic memories of your specific thing that derailed a day. The point is, life is not predictable, and as much as routines are very important for healthy living, being able to adapt to changing situations makes one successful. And autism and adaptability or flexibility are not exactly friends.

Situations where things are off, particularly when they are off beyond your control, can add a great deal of stress to the life of a person with autism. As we discussed earlier, being able to complete those routines is comforting and provides a sense of security. Not being able to do so produces anxiety and agitation, so that now the rest of the day may just be ruined, because you do not know what to expect. All of this takes place because you ran out of toothpaste!

The second aspect here I want to discuss is when you choose in advance to go off routine. Vacations are a prime example. You are going somewhere fun, but this involves staying at a hotel with a different setup. You took the travel toothpaste rather than the regular bottle as it would not go through TSA. Breakfast at a restaurant, no matter how many Michelin Stars it has, does not serve the preferred brand of microwave sandwich, and even if they did, the plate is different and the milk tastes different, or there are other people making noises.

Let me just pause here and acknowledge as a parent that this is really frustrating. For me, and this may be me over sharing, but I have lost it here. Sometimes I have lost it with an outward expression of anger (especially in the early days) which only makes things worse, but of late, it is just really discouraging when you are trying really hard to afford your child a wonderful experience, and have the whole day be ruined by something that (to me) seems so small. Although I have the intellectual capacity, professional training, and lived experience to understand what is going on, it sucks. And if you are reading this and are thinking how messed up I am because you have figured this out, please reach out and help me. However, it is frustrating when unavoidable changes to routines derail plans for family fun. Soon, we will further explore the topic of learning how to process these frustrations healthily.

To continue…maybe a beloved family member is staying with you, and as much as all love them, they don't know the unwritten rules related to when the bathroom is available or what seat is off limits at the table or living room. It could be a day off of school. A time when there is an expectation to sleep in and enjoy the morning, but there is a pre-dawn knock on your door wanting to know why you are not up. Sometimes you choose to go off routine for a good reason, but that choice opens the risk of unintended consequences.

ADHD

If we continue the analogy of southern cooking, if routines in autism are like the butter of southern cooking, for ADHD, routines are like Brussels sprouts (or any vegetable for that matter). They are really healthy for you, people tell you that you need them, but nobody anywhere wakes up in the morning and says, "Man, I wish I had me some Brussels sprouts right about now".

As much as those with ADHD very much so need routines to function healthily and prepare for the day, nothing about morning routines comes naturally for those with ADHD. In fact, even if you have autism and are fastidious about your morning routine, ADHD can easily distract a perfectly good routine with a toy you need to find, a game you want to play, or a squirrel playing in the backyard.

As we have mentioned, with ADHD there is a lack of motivation to do things you don't enjoy, and there is also the tendency to get easily distracted. More to come on this soon. So unless you really enjoy brushing your teeth and getting dressed (and maybe some do), it is usually not exciting or easy to get ready in the morning. Therefore, it is a challenge to get motivated to get your day started. Time-blindness also plays a role here with ADHD, as it is hard to judge how long it will take you to complete these tasks. And if you are thinking, "You do this every day, how do you not know how long it will take you to get ready," you are not alone. I should put that on a T-shirt!

A second element with ADHD is distractibility. Even if you are in a good place with a healthy morning routine, the distractions are real. Maybe a friend texted you, and you got sucked into a 20-minute text thread. Perhaps a song came on you liked and you just had to dance. Maybe the urge to just go irritate somebody else in the house was the dopamine boost you needed today. The dog brought you a ball, so you had to go play fetch. Whatever it is, you got distracted and now you are not ready. And because you did not get ready properly, you don't have any of the things you need to be successful today, so your whole day is shot. Might as well just go back to bed. It doesn't matter if you still have time to turn it around, you just go back to bed.

Adolescence

For adolescence, the degree to which one cares is very similar to heat in cooking. With too much heat, the food burns. Not enough heat, it will not get cooked. Some mornings, they care way too much. And caring too much about how one looks, how others might perceive how you look, being early, not eating too much, or not eating too little can be overwhelming. And before you know it, getting ready in the morning just got burned, because too much heat was applied. Maybe you can scrape the burned parts off and still make it, but sometimes not.

The flip side, and this is likely more prevalent in the male adolescent, but you just care too little. With hair that looks like the parent is one step away from having child protective services called on them for neglect. With no oversight, pajamas may still be on as they head out the door. If pajamas were exchanged for actual clothing, those clothes may or may not be clean. And what's that smell? "Oh well," they think, "nobody will notice that I smell like a skunk that got run over by a sewer truck, I can use a spritz of body spray."

And then, one day it happens. On a day you literally rolled out of bed last minute, your crush notices you and gives you a compliment. Then, the next day you wake up extra early to recreate the monstrosity of your appearance of the day before when you just rolled out of bed, but are not even getting close because now you care way too much!

This care in adolescence is not just care for self, but it is a care for how others are perceiving you. What other people think of and about you can be a precious commodity in adolescence. This will determine what social circles you get invited into, what clubs and activities you attend. In short, if people don't think of you how you think they should think of you, your life is ruined before it ever starts, or so you think. What is fascinating is how much people seem to be attracted to people who don't seem to care what others think about them. So, the trick is to look like you don't care, even though you really do. Everybody wants to be the person who just doesn't care, but unfortunately, almost everybody does.

A-hole

Speaking of not caring…this is the a-hole. The line is very slim between somebody who is the social ideal of not caring, and who is just an a-hole. In cooking terms, these are the people who can cook without a recipe. Some, like my grandma, just never had to measure things or look at a paper to know what to add. She just did it until it felt right. She could do this while mixing up dough, and her biscuits were amazing. I try it, and it is just a waste of ingredients.

Sometimes the a-hole does not care; other times they are actively trying to sabotage others. If I know we can't leave until I'm ready, then since I don't want to go, I'll just not get ready. If I know it ticks Mom off if I don't brush my teeth, I'm gonna not brush them just to prove a point. Dad hates this shirt, so I'm gonna wear it. If he makes me change it, then he is gonna be late for work.

This a-hole portion focuses on getting what you want, and causing distress to others makes it even better.

You are tired, so you just go back to bed after you wake up, or after someone kindly wakes you up. You want sleep. Never mind that you are tired because you refused to go to bed the night before; that's not your fault. You wanted to play your game last night. It's your mom's fault for waking you up, so you take out your tiredness and frustration on mom, or the toothbrush you fling around the bathroom, or the dog you yell at.

You don't want to go wherever you are getting ready to go. So you don't get ready. Never mind that everybody else has somewhere else to go; that's their problem. I'm just gonna do what I want to do.

For morning routines, even if you know the routine is good and healthy for you, some days you just don't care. Or, you use the lack of doing the routine as a weapon to inflict frustration on others who want you to complete healthy routines.

Suggestions

As with any of these suggestions offered, I don't know the details of your situation. Some things I suggest are just not going to work for you. But if something sounds interesting, try it.

1. Talk about expectations for what a healthy morning routine would look like. Define the parts of the routine. Things like

brushing teeth, combing hair, applying deodorant, washing face, picking up dirty clothes, throwing away trash, making bed, eating breakfast, etc.

2. Make the routine visible. This could be a chart on the wall and/or in the bathroom. It could also be associated with smart watches or electronic devices. It might be less of an emotional reaction when Alexa or Siri tells you to do something versus mom or dad.

3. Celebrate wins. When a routine is completed successfully, make a big deal out of it.

4. Model healthy routines. I can be hard to hear you over your actions;-). And if this is a struggle for you, admit it. Talk it through with your child and ask for their help in keeping you accountable.

5. Work with your child on mapping out how much time each item on their list might take. This can help them know how much time they need to complete these tasks. This can also be helpful in keeping them on task.

6. If you have timing figured out, multiple morning alarms labeled for each task could be a good non-parental prompt. This may work better than Mom or Dad reminding, especially if they set the alarms themselves. Remember, you won't always be there to help them, so they can use things like this when you are unavailable.

7. Be patient. You should be patient, especially when you feel frustrated. This will add extra negative energy to an already charged event. It is like bringing a candle to a gasoline spill.

8. Prep the night before. Get in the habit of morning routines beginning the night before. Whether it is bedtime impacting the next day, or selecting clothes, organizing backpacks/homework, returning shoes and watches and

wallets to their assigned locations. These help tie a thread that, in preparing the day before, it leads to success the day of. It is not a guarantee, but it removes a few variables.

9. Limit morning distractions. You can adjust internet routers to prevent internet access until a specific time, thus minimizing morning distractions. Set screen time locks so getting ready is the only activity available.

10. Have something you do together to prep for the day. Read a Bible passage, say a prayer, tell a joke, give an affirmation, or do something that can set a positive tone for the day.

Getting Ready to Leave

Besides morning routines, I want to take a few minutes to describe a related but slightly different scenario. There is an event that requires getting ready to leave at a certain time, but this trip is not a normal trip, like going to school, which happens every day at the same time. This one requires a little prep, but not like packing for a trip. And for the sake of illustration, let's just say your person is not excited about going. They do not oppose going, meaning they are not going to the dentist, but they could take it or leave it. Unfortunately, you can't leave them. They need to go with you.

Autism

For starters, this is not part of the normal routine. And since it is new or inconsistent, this trip will be disliked or feared. So the motivation to get ready is not there. And because it is new and unknown, special attention will need to be paid to securing the token, an item/toy used for comfort. You may or may not know, but just about every person on the spectrum will have something with them to soothe themselves. It's usually not something expensive or rare, but something that brings them comfort. A certain pen, a toy from a fast food meal, a sticker; it really could be anything. And God help you if it gets lost (more to come).

As you get closer and closer to the time you need to leave, and notice more and more that people are not in the car, you naturally repeat yourself that we need to go, and hope that repeating it louder will call attention to the importance of needing to hurry. However, the extra noise just negatively activates the sense, which results in a shutdown or a freak-out.

At this point, one of a few things is going to happen. One, you are not leaving on time and you are going to be late. Two, you may not even be going. Either you all stay home, or somebody stays home with your person. Three, if you manage to get people in the car, the recovery from the overstimulation will cause a miserable trip there, and possibly a miserable experience the whole time you are wherever you needed to be, which takes us back to number two, you might have wished you did not go to start with.

ADHD

This is hard for people without ADHD to understand what I am about to describe, but if you have ADHD and want to do something, the amount of focus or hyperfocus you can muster up is unparalleled. But if you don't want to do it, the sound of your own heartbeat can distract you. (Okay, if you have ADHD, check your heartbeat now and then come on back.)

Hear being okay? Great. Let's get back to it. Since there is no desire to go on this trip, there is no motivation to get ready. There is also a good chance that time-blindness will be on full display. You don't realize that it takes 15 minutes to get dressed, brush your teeth, put on your socks, put on your shoes, and gather your stuff. It's 3 minutes before it's time to leave, and you are still playing video games in your PJs, but think you still have plenty of time to get ready. In fact, it was the third time somebody yelled to get ready that lit the fire under you to recognize there is a crisis. And much like Smokey and the Bandit, you're "gonna do what they say can't be done." Which is to get dressed and ready in 3 minutes!

So you start out to get your stuff, like socks, and because you have autism, there is one pair of socks you like. And this trip to an unknown place will require your special socks, but you also have ADHD, so there is no telling where those socks are, or if they are even clean, since you wear them often. And in case you are keeping score at home, that sock hunt took 2 minutes. You still need to brush your teeth, comb your hair, and get dressed. Recognizing that you are out of time, you devise a plan. Your teeth don't need to be brushed, not like you are gonna make out with anybody, and you really don't care about your hair. But you will be in the car for a bit; you can just get dressed there. So you grab your clothes and shoes, and all you need is your token. Oh CRAP!! Where is your token? You were playing with it last night; you got out of the car in the garage, so maybe it is in the garage. You go look; it's not there. Panic is ensuing. Maybe it is in the kitchen. You got milk earlier, so it could be in the fridge. It's not there!! And now it's past the time to leave! People are yelling! It's not your fault you can't find your token. It was in your pocket earlier…oh wait, it's in your pocket. Off you go, a complete mess with clothes in tow, which may or may not be clean, but you are late. Again. Everybody is ticked off.

Adolescence

Why do we need to go? Why to I need to go? I don't even want to go. And my parents are gonna be there!? What if somebody I know sees me? Sees me with my parents?! This is going to knock me down a few points in my made-up social standing meter that I (and only I) know about. So if I have to go, I'd better look right. This is going to require a shower, which takes an exorbitantly long time. It is annoying that people keep beating on the bathroom door to use the bathroom, as I need this time both for getting ready and for rehearsing any social interactions that may transpire. And where better to do that than in the shower while I use up all the hot water I don't pay for, as it drowns out the noise of my annoying family, who keeps beating on the door telling me it's time to leave. I can't leave until I get properly dressed and ready.

Clothes. I have no acceptable clothes to wear. Nothing is clean, and what is clean is not folded (thank you, ADHD), and now I'm just going to get made fun of if I have to wear this. "Stop YELLING!" I'm gonna slam this door since he is yelling. I know what time it is. I can read a clock…a digital clock. Nobody born this century can read an analog wall clock. "FINE, I'M COMING!" I hate this family.

A-Hole

I'm not going. Try to make me go. And if I go, I'll make this the most miserable experience of your life. Try me, old man.

Summary

As you can see, this simple scenario that we face, needing to just simply leave in time, can be profoundly impacted or hijacked by any of our ingredients. And at every point in time, all are present. It really is like a four - way tug-of-war, or one of those soccer games with four teams and four goals, with a field full of people kicking multiple balls. On the outside, looking in, it's chaotic. But it is even worse on the inside looking out. From the outside, it may be possible to categorize these thoughts or behaviors, but for the one experiencing it, there is no reference for separating the various factors that are influencing or controlling you. It's just you, and this is everyday life.

Suggestions

So here are a few suggestions that sometimes work. I wish I could tell you they work all the time, but…please re-read the a-hole response. Sometimes you can't help if somebody does not want to get helped.

1. Talk about it in advance. Talk through the variables. Give time to look up the venue. Answer as many questions as you can.

2. Discuss the importance it has to you. Share this is a big deal and why it is important that you are on time.

3. Walk through a timeline of when things need to get done to be ready.

4. If it is really important, get their stuff ready for them. Lay out clothes, locate tokens, get all the chargers and such. And, pro-tip, put it in the car so it does not get lost.

5. Stay calm. No yelling.

6. Instruct people to be ready 15-30 minutes earlier than necessary to create a buffer and ensure you are not late.

7. Negotiate a treat for them if the trip is successful.

8. This gets a little nuclear, but shut down electronics and the internet 30 minutes before it's time to leave. This has several obvious and not so obvious risks associated with it, so use with care.

9. Give your kid a job to help others get ready.

10. Just stay home and tell people you have a vomit/diarrhea bug!! (Or, better yet, just contract a vomit/diarrhea bug so you can stay home!!)

Phone

Interacting with a smartphone is a pretty common occurrence. Almost everybody has one, and it is really convenient. In fact, every word typed on the original manuscript up to this point has been with my thumbs on a smartphone. But like most things that can make our life easier, if left unchecked, they can sometimes enslave us! So let's see how autism, ADHD, adolescence, and a-hole interact with phones.

Autism

For my son, I have understood that his phone is something he can control. While he has little control over other aspects of his life, his phone's elements are within his command. He can tell music where to stop and start. He can watch his preferred part of one scene of a video or a show over and over and over again. And when coupled with headphones, he can do this without distractions from others. He can truly be in his own world. His phone will do exactly what he tells it to do. It does not have emotions or sarcasm. It does not look at him funny when he asks it a random question; it simply responds. And when he is tired of it, he can put it down and walk away. He does not have to explain why he is done; he can just walk away. No social skills required.

It is also something that he uses as a compensatory skill. He is regularly asking Siri or Google to answer questions for him. And no matter what the question, it has an answer. Questions like, "How do I get my dad to let me go to the movies?" Or, "How do I know if a girl likes me?" Or, "what percent of toys are made in Vietnam?" AI (and despite that second letter being an "i" for the longest time he thought it was an "L" and called it Al like it was short for Albert) will spit out an answer. Sometimes, it is a brilliant answer. In trying to support his cause of going to a movie, he will read me AL's response and list all the reasons he should be able to go to a movie. And while it did not overcome the fact that he has no money because he spent it all (more to come on that), it has the potential to be a great tool for him to help navigate the confusing world around him.

But there is a cost to this. It's easy to get trapped in this world and forget that dealing with actual people is different. While it has the potential to enhance social skills, it can lull you into a false confidence that the digital reality is reality. And you lose functionality in the real world.

And then there are the internet trolls. While some go to cyberspace with altruistic motives, some are there to manipulate and abuse others; being mean for their own pleasure or personal gain. And for a person on the spectrum, it can be really hard to separate truth from lies, kindness from deception.

And if we are being honest, it's not just those on the spectrum who fall prey. As our media outlets become more siloed and partisan, it's easy to get convinced that what is being presented is the truth, as little fact-checking occurs. This is not a cut on any political party, because it happens on both sides. You get so stuck in your own opinion, and you find outlets that reinforce your own opinion so you no longer consider any other options. Only your way is right and everybody else is stupid.

If we do this with neurotypical brains, how much more so is this happening to those on the spectrum who lack the ability to interpret those micro clues of social interactions!

ADHD

Whenever I am on a road trip and am driving on a long, straight, 2 lane road, it gets hard to stay awake. I can easily get board with the never-ending pine tree that I keep seeing. Before long, it is easy to just nod off. I am the weirdo who truly enjoys the traffic of a big city. Put me in Miami, Orlando, or Atlanta when the road goes from 2 lanes to 10, with random road signs describing a spaghetti of exits, construction, a carpool lane, and crazy drivers from all over the world, and I get locked in. I am awake, alert, and focused.

I imagine the use of a phone for those with ADHD is like me hitting big-city traffic. There is just enough going on with a phone that it can fully engage an ADHD brain. There are multiple apps that can all be open at the same time, games that provide visual, audio, and tactile stimulation, and all of this while you are listening to your music, texting your friends, and scrolling social media, and taking videos of yourself. FINALLY, something can keep up with you. If it were not for that one annoying sound, this would be perfect. Wait, that annoying sound keeps getting louder and more frequent. What is Mom doing here and what is she saying? You take out an earbud to an angry tirade from mom who is yelling your name and going off like she has been yelling for a while. I have not been on my phone for 3 hours…wait, what time is it? Was Mom the annoying sound disrupting my peace? Where is that earbud I just took out of my ear? It's all Mom's fault I lost it!

The phone can be a tremendous tool for those with ADHD. It can be used to set alarms for important times, notes and reminders to stay organized, and calendars can be a tremendous help. There are apps that can even help improve focus. But like many good things, there are also temptations, and one of those temptations is to just escape. And very little can engage hyperfocus like a phone or a video game. And when the video game is on the phone, "At last…my love has come along". It can be the perfect blend that just helps your brain go to its happy place.

And much like in our discussion with autism, it is not just those with ADHD who can get caught in its trap. Neurotypicals and atypicals alike can easily use a phone as a happy place to lull us from the torments of everyday life. Whether that be a good cat video, some candy that needs crushing, or a bird with anger issues, it can be a welcome retreat.

While there are options for the phone to help improve focus, the constant short-term stimulation, the constant change of the reel, and the quick flip between apps, can all work together negatively to decrease focus. Our brains get to where they yearn for the commercial interruption because the main show is already being tuned out. Advertisers pay professionals a lot of money to determine the optimal length of an interval for maximum commercial impact. While kids today, by default, have to multitask in ways we never dreamed of "back in the day", their ability to stay focused on a single task without getting distracted does not come as easily to them, as they have never had to stare out of a car window at clouds on a road trip.

Adolescence

I waited in line at the Apple Store, standing in the July sun for several hours in 2008 for my first iPhone 3. My oldest was 2, my youngest was -1. My kids have never lived in a world without smartphones. It is hard for those of us who grew up without smartphones to fully understand the all-encompassing impact this one machine has on the daily social life of an adolescent. When I was a kid, I had breaks from my social circles. Yeah, I had AOL chats, but that involved a wired-phone line, a dial-up modem, and it took some intentionality and planning to talk with friends there. The closest thing we had to text messaging involved a beeper. (I feel like I'm gonna go into a Cracker Barrel and see things like a beeper, a modem, a wired phone, and a VHS player on the wall soon!) All that to say, I was not constantly connected. My parents could not track me. They had to trust me. My friends had to call my house to speak to me on the phone, the phone that was connected to the wall by a wire. If you wanted to send somebody a written message, it involved a pen and paper. And emojis were those people who wore all black…wait, those were emos.

For today's adolescent, the phone (and all the social media apps it contains) is best understood not so much as an accessory but as an appendage. It is a part of you. If a social crisis happens on the phone, it does not stay in the phone. It has happened to you. Being without it is like putting a patch over one eye or plugging an ear. It limits your functionality. So much can happen so quickly on a phone, and to not be on it and engaged with it will render you a social outcast if you don't respond or react in a timely fashion. Or so they lead you to believe.

For example, if news breaks that somebody has done something horrendous, and you don't immediately denounce their evil, others will take your lack of denouncement as an endorsement of their evil, and it won't be long until you are accused of being supportive of it, engaged in it, or an accomplice to the evil. In phone-world, you are not innocent until proven guilty; the accusation alone is enough to ruin you. And if someone accuses you, your friends must immediately denounce and unfriend you, or they will fall prey to the same fate.

So when you take a phone from your adolescent as a punishment, and your adolescent begs you to take a belt and beat them instead, they are not lying. A whipping is easier to recover from than the amputation of having a phone removed.

As much as I would like to say phones are not a necessary part of life…they are quickly becoming essential. More and more businesses are assuming you have them. Many restaurants no longer have paper menus; they just put a QR code on the table, partly to save costs and partly to more easily adjust prices! Theme parks all but require mobile ordering, and even payment for parking your car requires a phone.

How can you help your adolescent survive and thrive in a world where phones seem to be completely integrated into their lives? More to come, but we have one more "A"spect to consider when considering actions related to the phone.

A-hole

There seem to be two categories here. One where you have a choice, and one where you have surrendered your choice. One needs discipline; the other needs treatment.

When things are intentionally being hidden on a phone, this is an a-hole problem. Meaning, you are deleting texts, hiding apps, using multiple accounts on the same platforms, basically trying to avoid accountability. Some may even have a separate, secret phone. This is when you are likely being an a-hole with a phone. And whether or not you are hiding your identity, whenever you start to be a bully or a troll to someone, this is a-hole behavior.

But this is another type of a-hole that differs from what we are describing. This is when you are addicted to your phone. You can't put it down or ignore it. You must keep the streak alive. The phone is more important than people or relationships. No matter how much you are on it, it is never enough. This is an addiction.

Not everybody who drinks alcohol is a drunk, and not everybody who uses a phone is an addict. But when you don't have limits, and the use impairs your functioning in other areas, it may be time to think through the response differently. But this can get complicated. If your kid were an alcoholic, you would not hand them a beer every morning. You would get rid of all the alcohol, or at the least lock it up. But for those with a digital addiction, handing them a phone every day is not wise or loving. But they might legitimately need their phone. How else will you know where they are? How else will they do their homework? Complicated!

My goal here is not to make sweeping statements, as there are no single right answers. I bring this up as a way of showing there may need to be a different way to think about this. And if you are not helping to set limits proactively, addiction is a possibility.

Suggestions

The following serve as conversation starters. Each situation and person is different, so no judgement here. But if you are looking for some place to start, I propose the following.

1. Before you give a phone, talk about its benefits and dangers. Make regular phone check-ins a normal part of the experience.

2. Model healthy phone usage. Don't expect your kids to do something you are unable or unwilling to do.

3. Learn (or hire someone to teach you) the various parental control options available with your phone's operating system. And set limits. Set limits on overall usage time and set specific limits for the time certain apps or categories can be used. Limit contacts, communication capabilities to strangers in games/apps, abilities to download and delete apps, and adult content. Basically, limit anything you can limit. While I could tell out how to do this on today's device, an update to the operating system tomorrow will change this. So you really need to do your homework, or hire someone to do it for you.

4. Check phones. Even if all is going well, and especially when all is going well, check phones. Make accountability normal. The more your kid knows you are going to check, the less likely they will be to try something. It is more about

catching them doing right and building trust than it is catching them doing wrong.

5. Ask questions. Know what they are doing on their phones. Favorite games, friends they are talking to, the music they are listening to, etc. Their phone is a part of them, so knowing what they are doing with it and where they are engaging with can help you get to know them better.

6. Establish consequences for poor phone behavior well in advance. This way, they know what will happen when they break the rules. If there is enough maturity, set the rules with them so they are breaking their own rules and the consequences are not something a mean parent is doing. This is a great life skill if your kid has the awareness to take part in this.

7. Set up phone-free zones. Maybe this is at dinner, or on certain car rides, or during a movie night. The trick is to get the adults to go phone-free as well!

8. When there are missteps, remember you are training them to use a device that will probably be a part of their everyday life for the rest of their lives. So think of discipline when it relates to the phone in terms of teaching and guiding rather than punishing.

9. Have them participate in the costs of the device and the service it requires. This may start out with them paying a portion. This is not to make money on your kid for providing cell service, but to help them understand the costs involved and that it is not free.

10. Periodically, discuss how the phone has improved your life instead of making all conversations about it negative. Share some stories from the dark-analog days before phones. Talk about how you had to do math in your head, AAA trip tickets and learning how to read maps when you traveled,

tell them about how long it took to get photos developed and how a stamp was involved to send messages. If you are always negative towards something that is such a major part of their lives, you risk that negativity being taken personally and ultimately losing credibility.

Finances

Everybody needs money, and although the gaining and spending of money is almost universal, people have different ideas of what money is and how to spend it. In the marriage counseling I have professionally conducted, managing finances is a frequent topic of discussion. In any premarital counseling I do, this is at least an entire session. It has the potential to be an issue for those with no neurological struggles, and autism, ADHD, adolescence, and being an a-hole is not exempt. Let's examine how each might interact with finances, and then we can talk about some suggestions.

Autism

Money is an abstract concept. Meaning, it involves a good bit of interpretation and symbols. All of which rarely play nice with autism. What makes pictures of dead people I draw on green paper in art class different from pictures of dead people on the bills in your wallet? Why does one have value and one does not? Why is one of your bills worth one dollar and another worth one hundred dollars, when they are the same size and same color? And this is the more concrete/tangible aspect of money.

When you deal with debit cards and online bank apps, it can feel like a video game. It is almost as if this money is not real. Just something that somebody made up. And if it's imaginary, why can't someone create more for me when I want/need it. I can get coins in my game by unlocking a level. Maybe it is like that in real life? If I roam around enough, perhaps I'll find more!

Another area where I see challenges with money for those with autism is understanding value. What makes something a good deal? If I want something, and there is enough money in my account to buy it, I don't see the problem with using what I have to get what I want. I really don't care if it is cheaper somewhere else. I'm not somewhere else; I'm right here and so is this item, and I want it. So why not spend whatever it takes to get what I want?

There really does not seem to be a correlation to how much work or time it took to get the funds in your account, and whether the thing you are getting ready to purchase is worth the amount of hours it took you to secure the funds to get what you want. And in my experience, there is not much of a care about how much something costs. I have watched my son spend $3 on a toy at a thrift store and enjoy it for weeks. It is a great expense. I have also seen him pay $15 for a drink at a theme park because it looked cool, take two sips, decide he does not like it, and then throw it away.

And because there is little understanding of value, when funds run out, and daily wants/needs still exist, there seems to be no awareness that money was spent poorly, which led to this. There also seems to be little connection to how this money gets into one's account. I have heard him say he will just call the bank and have them put money in his account. What tends to (unfortunately for me) yield better results is calling a grandparent to get money put into his account. That one works more times than not. Thankfully, thus far in our experience, credit cards are not part of the equation. I can only imagine how much more challenging the offer of what appears to be free money to spend now on what you want could bring financial ruin quickly.

Routines are to be considered here as well. If you bought something during your previous visit to the location, you must purchase that same item again today to complete the routine. For example, if the normal meal at the fast-food restaurant is a chicken sandwich with no pickles, fries and a Dr Pepper, if you stop only wanting to get a chicken sandwich because you are going home and drinks are at home, not buying the Dr. Pepper will create conflict. Not because he really wants the Dr. Pepper, but because he did not complete the routine.

ADHD

Impulse control is a major aspect of ADHD. What differs slightly from autism is that with ADHD it is more than a want; purchasing something seems to be an itch that needs to be scratched, or a soothing salve that needs to be placed on an open sore.

Insecurity and ADHD hang out together way too much. So the purchase could be an attempt to overcome an insecurity. If you could just buy this one (fill in the blank: outfit, toy, food item, etc.), then it will make up for the loss or lack you are feeling. So making that purchase feels like life or death. Not buying it will further propel you into oblivion. And, before you as the parent/guardian cite examples of how the previous 15-20 such purchases that are currently strewn all over their room, this one is different. This is the one that they HAVE to have.

And to offset the cost of the item, they will do some work later to make up for it. Until later gets there and ADHD kicks in and they forget to go to work, show up late, or just get distracted and don't do their chores. Not that somebody intends to not do the work in the future, in that moment they really would plan to do it. But when the time comes to put their mouth where your money went, that work is likely hard and not enjoyable, making it more and more challenging to accomplish that task. As a result, you are always chasing to catch up. And when you add credit cards to this, if you only need to make the minimum payment, who cares if you will never get out of debt. That is tomorrow's problem.

Adolescence

Social pressures are a major influence on finances. If everybody has a certain item, you may not want it, but you might need it to fit in. Having the cheaper off-brand item that functions in the same way is a great way to get left out of desired relationships and activities. While our natural tendency is to say no to any such purchase, I'd encourage you to hear your adolescent out. It may not make sense to you, but their reasoning may be pretty good. You may look at this purely in financial terms, but they may see it as an investment in a relationship. It could be a cool opportunity to discuss return on investment. Financial returns are not the only returns.

Besides social pressures, the invincibility of adolescence also plays a role in finances. If you are not familiar with this, that is the part of adolescence that says, "It will not happen to me!" So while others go broke making dumb financial decisions, "It will not happen to me". Besides, if an adolescent spent all their money, Mom and Dad will bail them out. Mom and Dad have credit cards! That is like magical money you never have to pay back! They can't wait until they turn 18 and can get one of those cards and buy whatever they want!

Increasingly, adolescents tend not to understand how much things cost or how money works. Does your adolescent know the cost of the mortgage/rent, the car payment, the grocery bill, the electric bill, the water/utility bill, the bill at Chick-fil-A for the family to eat, or your salary? Do they know principles of cash flow or debt, and how much interest impacts things? I'm aware that some of these are subjects we prefer not to address with our kids, or even our spouses. We want to help our kids grow up carefree. Maybe your parents lorded some of this over you, so you are trying to protect your kids. While I'm not suggesting that we make our financial struggles our kids' responsibility, some awareness could help with context to determine whether or not a purchase makes sense. Especially with the changes to our economy post-COVID, things are different. We know they are different, but they don't. While post-COVID has been an exception to us, it is all they have known. $15 at a fast-food restaurant is a normal cost for a meal, but what they don't realize is that salaries have not grown in proportion to prices.

A-Hole

In order to consider if an a-hole is active, the key factor is where or not there is an understanding of the reality of the financial situation. They know that a purchase is unnecessary or unrealistic, but demand it anyway. Why? Because they want it and don't care about anybody else. Maybe you sacrificed to take a special trip, spent money you did not have to make a memory, only to have your a-hole complain the whole time they were there that the hotel could have been better, the food was not as good, and you needed to stay longer to really enjoy it.

Or, you buy the thing that you can't afford to make them happy, and a day later you find it strewn on the floor or in the trash. They did not respect or appreciate it as you thought they would, and they did not treat it how you would have treated something of great value. Note, with autism, they may not know the value, but the a-hole knows. They are just selfish and don't care about others.

There is an assumption that others will just care for them. They will always get what they want. This is very similar to the invincibility of adolescence, but the a-hole aspect is more present when there seems to be a recognition that this is costing somebody something, but they just don't care. For example, a recent debate on student loans can illustrate the point. For some, they do not know how much debt they racked up, or who will be impacted if they don't pay that back. That's adolescence talking. For others, they knew good and well they would never get a job that would afford them a salary to pay back the loan in the overly expensive major they chose from a high-priced exclusive college, and they recognize everyday people will have to pay for their poor decisions, but they just don't care. They deserve to get what they want, no matter who pays for it. That's a-hole. This statement does not intend to start a political debate, but it illustrates the difference. Both adolescents and a-holes may ask for the same thing (in this case, debt forgiveness), but the separator has to do with their capacity to understand the implications.

Suggestions

Here are a few things to consider with finances. As with any suggestion, your own child's individual needs may determine how applicable some of these suggestions are. If your issue is autism, for example, explaining value may not be realistic as they are likely to never understand it. But this could be really helpful to your adolescent. So we will include some that may be compensatory skills they will just have to learn.

1. Talk about money. Don't fight about money. Just make talking about it normal. If you are looking for a place to start this conversation, https://www.moneyhabitudes.com is a great resource. This program helps you sort out your attitudes and habits towards money. You can see pretty quickly how your values may differ as you discover what money means to you and your child. It can really help frame a discussion on money.

2. Set a budget. Dave Ramsey has some great resources here. One thing we tried was helping kids plan a weekend activity. We gave them a budget they needed to stay under for the entire weekend. Suddenly getting water at a restaurant became a good idea so they would have enough money to do one more activity!

3. A cash envelope system is a good option for those who need things to be tangible. Get cash, all in the same denomination, like all $5s or $1s, and separate categories of the budget you created with one envelope per item. Once you spend all the money in your envelope on vending machines, you can't take money out of the clothes envelope to buy more from the vending machine. It is a great way to learn how to set money aside for the things you need, without letting the things you want get in the way.

4. Share your struggles and successes with money. Talk about purchases you made that you later regretted. Share the great deals you made. Just because you have messed up with money does not mean your kids have to follow in your footsteps. Use your mistakes to help them grow. History does not have to repeat itself. You don't have to have a perfect financial past to have the authority to speak about wise ways to use money.

5. As mentioned already, share the realities of household finances when it is age and cognitively appropriate. Even if you don't share dollar amounts, show a pie chart of what percentages of your household income goes where each month. This can help them gain perspective.

6. Help them get jobs. Teach them to work. If you want money, work is a great place to go. This can start with household chores, but get them into the actual workforce. For those with disabilities, there are often state-run programs like Vocational Rehab or other non-profits that can teach job skills. And while it may be inconvenient for you to get them to and from a job, it is a powerful skill to instill that work is good. It will also help with assigning value. Instead of something costing X dollars, you can frame it in terms of Y hours you spent working to get X dollars.

7. Teach and model living on less than you make. Teach them to give away 10%, 10-20% to savings, then live on the rest. This is not a magical formula, but is a great way to instill the principles of generosity, saving, and good stewardship.

8. Celebrate their financial successes. If they reach a goal and save a certain amount they planned to save, make a big deal. If they get a great deal, make a big deal about it.

9. If value is something they just can't get, set up checks and balances. Meaning, set a dollar amount they can't spend over without approval. This dollar amount will be different for you and for the situation, but you my go to a mall and say, you can buy any one thing you want as long as you don't spend more that X. If they want something that is more than X, they need to call for approval. This can help instill these compensatory skills for later in life. They may always need an external check; they may not. (You may also need this for you, just say'n, or rather your spouse is just say'n!)

10. If it looks like your person may not be able to handle their own money, you may need to set up guardianship over their finances so they do not make unnecessary financial messes.

School

There are so many aspects of school, and it can be overwhelming for just about anybody, students and teachers alike! For the discussion here, I want to focus on 2 specific aspects of school: academics and social interactions. Let's explore how each of our elements might interact with these two important aspects of school.

Autism

School is very routine. From the beginning of the day to the end, and in every class, the timings and your seating are predictable. For some, this can be very comforting. And the world of academia can be a strong suit for some on the spectrum. Right and wrong answers, absolutes, can soothe the autistic mind. But as you get older, and subjects delve into the nuances of literature, and require interpreting history rather than producing facts and dates, school can get more challenging.

But academics is just one aspect of school. Social interactions are a completely different animal for kids with autism. Social pressures are challenging, but even more so when you have documented and diagnosed deficits with social situations. When this is the case, school can be isolating or just plain miserable. Spending 8 hours a day with nobody to connect with, and trying to avoid getting bullied can be draining. There seem to be 2 camps here. Some experience this, and because they never really want or seek social interaction, it is not that big of a deal. But the other camp is when they want to connect, and as much as they might try, just can't. And while most would experience this as sadness, some on the spectrum at not be able to process this emotion. So it may come out as anger, aggression, and a flat-out refusal to go to school.

What I have learned is that when my child is reacting in a way that does not seem appropriate, I need to investigate further. There is likely a cause, but the reason for this reaction that makes perfect sense to my child does not line up with my logic. For example, he was getting home from elementary school and was just furious. We could not figure it out. There were no issues that his teachers were telling us about. We asked him; he did not have a reason for what was happening. It was a few weeks later that we found out another student was bullying him on the bus ride. This was really bothering him, and he just did not have the ability to tell us he was being mistreated on the bus. Instead, he was agitated when he got home.

ADHD

Academics require attention and focus that are in short supply already. And unless the subject is engaging (the teacher can go a long way here), school, for those with ADHD, can be a real challenge. To be successful in an environment that is very much so not catered to your needs requires an abundance of energy being spent on compensatory skills. Think of it this way: it's like the refrigerator trying to keep your food cold with the door open all day. It can do it for a while, but eventually the motor will burn out.

While academics can be difficult by itself, it is even more compounded by the social scene at school. For many with ADHD, they are the life of the party. The comic relief amid an otherwise unenjoyable experience. The drive to break up the monotony is extreme, and the positive social reinforcement received for doing so makes whatever consequences (poor grades, disciplinary actions) easily worth it.

After all, who needs school anyway? All these chumps are gonna work for you someday, as you are the only one with the risk tolerance necessary to consider starting a business. And with your personality and people skills, it's likely to grow. You will hire these nerds to do all the nerd stuff while you are enjoying your life and sticking it to the man, whoever he is.

Adolescence

Developmental levels can be a very significant influence on school performance, both academically and socially. During middle and high school, students are increasingly being exposed to subjects that require formal operational thinking. The hope and goal is that by introducing these concepts to kids early, they can develop greater mastery and be more successful in college and life.

The problem is, until your brain develops to where you can access this higher level of functioning, you will not be successful with certain subjects. Asking an undeveloped brain to do algebra is like mounting a boat motor on the trunk of a car. It will crank up and spin, but it's not going anywhere because it is not in water!

And there are some downstream (yes, that pun was intended) impacts of this. When, for example, a student who was great in math when it was about addition/subtraction/multiplication /division gets into an algebra class and just cannot understand who X is and why he and Y can't get along and constantly needs to be found, it can really mess with one's view of self. You can lose confidence, develop anxiety and depression, and before long you act out to help you avoid going to class. Parents often wonder what has happened to their sweet kid who was great in elementary school. Sometimes, it can just be a developmental issue. Your kid's brain may not be ready for some of the higher-level classes the school is pushing them into.

And while we are at it, not every career is going to require formal operational thinking. This does not mean that people are dumb if they can't three-dimensionally graph an equation; it means that God gifted them differently and that they can be extremely successful in a career path that matches their aptitude. I believe our schools do an injustice by pushing high-level academics that may never be useful for some career paths.

Developmental levels also play a tremendous role in social circles. If you begin puberty at 9 or 10 (that might be 3rd grade!!) but your friends don't enter puberty until they are 13 (potentially 8th grade), you are going to stand out. The flip side of this is also true if you are on the later side of puberty. I believe this is particularly more challenging for girls, mainly because of the over-sexualization of our society. When a girl 11 years old has feminine features that are consistent with those of a 22-year-old, it can have profound impacts on social interactions. Either you are the most popular person in school, or everybody hates you because they are not you, or both at the same time! And because you are constantly being admired sexually, this can lead to over-sexualized behaviors, or a complete aversion to sex because you are so fed up with people always talking about this.

For guys, this often plays out on a sports field. If you are on a middle school football team and the guy across from you has a full beard and body odor, but puberty is nowhere close to you, it is going to be hard to compete. And in our sports-crazed culture, this can have profound social implications.

Developmental levels are totally out of one's control, but can lay foundations for identity and connection that will follow you for life. Along with development come hormone changes. And in school, for those whose bodies are developing sexual organs, school can be a place of tremendous sexual tension. Historically, by the time you developed sexually, you were getting married and having sex. But now, you can develop sexually at 10, but don't get married until your late 20s! So sitting in a classroom next to somebody who is also sexually developing with the same urges and hormones you have can make focusing on history almost impossible! And if you engage in activities your body has developed the capacity for, your brain has not developed enough to handle these bonds and connections. You may bond with somebody sexually, but the intellectual and emotional bonds are not mature enough to sustain this type of relationship. So when you break up, it is emotionally similar to getting a divorce, with none of the legal or societal support that getting a divorce would offer.

In therapy sessions, I frequently saw depressed and almost suicidal adolescents who had just gone through a breakup. Almost always, those relationships were sexual. The breakup created a loss they were just not equipped to handle emotionally because the bond that sex created was so strong, as the bond of sex is supposed to be.

These are only two elements of adolescence and school. We have not even touched on the social media aspect of school. While we have mentioned this in other places, please keep in mind that having every moment of an adolescent's life potentially recorded and shared is a social pressure that adolescents of yesteryear never had to experience. The stress, the pressure, the anxiety, the depression…it is real. And it impacts academic and social functioning, and a bunch of other areas of functioning we have not even discussed.

A-Hole

While there may be some who are just horrible people and just find great pleasure in being a-holes, I am going to be a little kinder in this section to our a-hole friends. Sure, some are just mean and selfish and only care about themselves. This is a pretty consistent theme with a-holes. But given what we have discussed with developmental levels and social media pressures, a-holes may only have little options when it comes to school.

For example, if you developed later, you likely do not understand what is going on in a majority of your classes. Raising one's hand and admitting you are clueless rarely creates empathy in the minds of your friends and teachers to help you. It is a prime way to get made fun of. It is not a long leap to figure out that no matter what you do; you are going to be a social outcast because you just can't keep up. And there is not a lot you can do to keep up. So you need a new identity, and you need it fast. So when you are behind in class, you need to own your own narrative, and you decide to be a jerk. You make fun of others before they can make fun of you. Because you are small, you might have to be mean to survive. While it may start out as a temporary fix, before long, it has become your brand, and now you have a following; a standing in society. And while you may not want to be an a-hole, it has become your identity. And, as much as you hate to admit it, you kinda like the notoriety it has given you.

On the other end of this spectrum, if you have developed very early, you really have no equal in school. Things are just easy for you. Academics you understand, and you are sick and tired of these fools asking dumb questions for content you clearly understand. You are board, so to spice things up, you make fun of dumb people. It breaks up the boredom, and people kind of think it is funny. But are they laughing because you are the most physically developed person in your grade and they are afraid of you, or do they really like you? You may never know for sure, but at least they are focused on something other than your physical appearance for a second, and that feels good.

Or, perhaps you were one of those early developers and you had all the attention to yourself for several months or maybe even an entire year or two, and you really liked it. You were popular and interesting. Everybody wanted to talk to you. But now, others have started to develop physically. You are no longer the only game in town. Others are competing for attention that was previously yours alone. You must do something to get that back. So the quickest way to get attention is to get negative attention. That will get you likes and follows if you learn how to tear somebody down, and bonus points if you can do it publicly or online. You are back! People want to know what you think and people want to talk to you. It may be out of fear that you won't tear them down and not because they are actually your friend, but who cares. You again have the attention that you need.

It is still a choice that you make to lead the life of an a-hole, but sometimes it is as though you feel backed into a corner, and this was the best of your bad options. It is hard to think beyond the present in adolescence. You don't care about yourself in 5 years when high school is over; you just want to survive today. And sometimes, being an a-hole is the least bad of your bad options.

And we have not even touched on those who have been through adverse childhood experiences. Things like abuse, neglect, domestic violence, not having enough money, death in the family, parents getting a divorce, feeling unloved, somebody in your family going to jail, bullies, racism, mental illness, or any number of childhood traumas. Trying to explain all of this to somebody when you don't even understand it for yourself can make being an a-hole attractive, as it keeps people from knowing the real you. That is way too vulnerable, and you learned early on that vulnerability equals weakness, and weakness leads to pain. So if you can put up the a-hole exterior, you can build a wall around all that trauma. And that might be a good survival tactic for now until you forget to build a door in your wall and realize later in life that you have just trapped yourself in a box you built! (Sorry, that's the therapist in me coming out.)

Sometimes there is more to being an a-hole than selfishness. Sometimes it is the only option your undeveloped brain can come up with to protect you. It is just really unfortunate for those around you, and even more unfortunate for the person who is hurting and needing help, but has built intense barriers to getting that help or receiving it. It can take a long time to knock a few holes in that wall later in life to eventually build a door to let some of the toxic waste out and allow some help to clean things up.

Individualized Education Plans

If this is not you, please skip this section. Trust me, as one who has to attend IEP meetings, I really wish I could skip this. But many on this journey have questions about Individualized Education Plans, or IEPs. While the processes are a little different in each school district, I want to mention it as this has the potential to be a big part of your school journey. This does not aim to provide a step-by-step guide for maximizing IEPs. There are just too many differences from district to district, and certainly from state to state. But I want to give you a general idea of what an IEP is and how you can get some additional help.

In its most basic form, an IEP is a way for a student who is struggling to stay on grade level by having an individual plan to be successful. You will find this more in public schools than you will in private schools. Not every kid who struggles needs an IEP, but schools enact the IEP to fill in the gaps when your kid has documented delays or difficulties and is consistently behind.

Typically, teachers need to prove (with data) that your kid is not performing on grade level. They will often try several attempts in the classroom to help a child who is behind to get on grade level. After making those attempts and proving with data that it does not work, then the conversation about an IEP usually comes up.

I come from a family of teachers. My mom was a teacher, my wife is a teacher, and her mom was a teacher. I express what I am about to say with love and respect for teachers, but teachers vary in their skills and talents. The process of getting a child approved for an IEP and special/exceptional education services is very complicated and time-consuming, and universities rarely teach it. This is something teachers need to learn how to do on their own. And even when they know what to do, it is a significant amount of paperwork and documentation. And unlike most normal jobs, they get paid nothing more to do all of this extra work. In fact, it somewhat punishes them to do it, as it takes time away from other tasks they have to complete. So either they are behind in their normal work to help get your kid the help they need, or they have to take work home and work un-paid after hours. I say this to help you partner with your child's teacher and not just show up and complain to the teacher/principal/school. Advocate for your kid, but advocate with their teacher as a partner. Don't run roughshod over the teacher in the process. You don't want the one person who spends the most time with your kid other than you angry and irritated at you or your kid!

Providing these types of services is very expensive for a school district. So there is a reason they need to have the data to prove that the expense is necessary. For this reason, schools do not pass out an IEP to every kid who makes a poor grade on a test. Sometimes, they got a poor grade because they did not study, or did not sleep well the night before, or were too busy focusing on the attractive person next to them and not their test. This is not a reason to give somebody an IEP. The data has to show that it is a consistent and pervasive issue that requires a more involved intervention than what the teacher can reasonably provide in the classroom.

There are numerous accommodations available for kids with autism and ADHD. Learn what those are for your district. Programs like CARD (Center for Autism Related Disorders) and CHADD (Children and Adults with Attention-Deficit/Hyperactivity Disorder) can be great resources. There are also professional IEP advocates that may be worth the money to talk to, as they can help you navigate some of the red tape. These advocates can also help you better understand what accommodations can be offered by your district. Things like extra time to complete tests, having test questions read to them, various seating accommodations to help kids who need to fidget in their seats, or weighted vests to feel more comfortable. There are several ways that schools can help your child be successful. Get knowledge of what is available. It is highly likely that your kid's teacher may not know what these options are, unless they just have a passion for working with kids with needs. This does not make them a terrible teacher; it just means they have not had exposure to specialized needs and accommodations. If they possess expert knowledge of what can be offered to your child, buy them dinner and take notes.

Most of the time, this process starts in elementary school. It is a process to get a kid qualified for an IEP, and it takes work to advocate for what is on the IEP and constantly meet to discuss the IEP. While you may not be starting this process in adolescence, there is a good chance you will have to monitor and adjust the plan as your child develops and encounters different struggles and abilities in adolescence. So here is a tip for making the most of an IEP meeting. When you get to school meetings, declare it an acronym-free zone. In education circles, it gets easy to just speak in acronyms. And if you are not in that world, you do not know what they are talking about. I went to a school meeting once (at the high school) as part of a special focus group for special needs parents. Besides my kid's teachers being there, there were the principal and someone from the state. When the state person started waxing eloquent in acronyms, I raised my hand and asked her to tell me what a few acronyms stood for, and she could not. They had to Google it, and it turns out there is an entire webpage on the State of Florida's education department's website devoted solely to school acronyms. I recommended the equivalent of a swear jar, where we had to put in a quarter every time somebody used an acronym. They did not like that idea! My point here is you are not dumb if you don't understand the specialized language that school personnel are using, because they don't understand it either sometimes. Make them tell you this in plain language. You and your child deserve to understand what is being presented to you.

Don't just sign things you don't understand because you don't want to feel stupid; you are no longer in high school. Ask the questions. Make them explain to you what they want you to sign. And if you don't understand it, don't sign it. Tell them you need to take it with you and read through it more and get some help. They won't like it, but you have every right to do this. You also have the right to bring people with you to these meetings to help you out. This is where an IEP advocate can be really helpful.

Suggestions

School is a complex topic. The higher you are in school, the more complex it is. So if your kids are young, some of these suggestions will be easier to implement. If they are older, some may not apply. But please understand that school today is not what you experienced. The more you can seek to understand the perspective of your child, the better the opportunity exists to not just survive in school, but to thrive.

1. Communicate with your child. Ask questions. Open-ended questions and ask them from different angles. "How was school" is not one of those questions you should ask. But questions like, "What made you laugh today?", or "Who was a jerk to you today?", or "What was the most exciting thing that happened today?", are better questions. Understand that school is not only about academics. Get to know the other aspects of school.

2. Know your child's limits and abilities. Resist the urge to enroll your child in everything. Your kid needs to rest, and you do too. You don't have to enroll your child in a higher-level course just because it's offered. They will not wind up homeless because they did not take an AP class. If your kid has an IEP or some type of accommodation, know what is in that paperwork and advocate for your kid. Nobody else can fight for your kid to be successful like you can.

3. Talk with the school. Don't be that jerk parent, but communicate with the teachers. Buy coffee for your kid's teacher. Read the papers they send home. Reach out to them through the channels they offer for you to connect with them. These people are with your kid for a significant portion of their day. And they are people too, with their own hurts and hangups, and they are likely getting paid significantly less than what they are worth. So reach out and partner with them. Be a resource and not an obstacle. Make it so that when they see an email from you or get a phone call from you, they are excited about it and do not have to engage in breathing exercises to deal with you!

4. Get involved in the school. Volunteer in the classroom. Attend field trips. Be the supportive parent for the after-school activity. If your kid won't tell you what is going on, maybe their friends will!

5. Know that school is more than academics. Speak life into the other areas of school that are less tangible and don't receive a report card. Your kid needs you and your guidance on this.

6. Know your kid's friends. The friends in real life and the friends in digital life. See who they are following. Know who they are chatting with in games.

7. Help your kids gain perspective. Share with them how school experiences have shaped you. Talk about the friendships you value today from your time in school, and the ones that you don't value. They will not understand this as they may comprehend nothing but the present, but you are laying foundations for their development.

8. Teach and model boundaries. Help your kids know what the limits are in a physical relationship. Know the limits of financial transactions. Place a high importance on getting

sleep and proper nutrition. This will not only help them survive school but thrive in life.

9. Be silly. In all the stress and pressure of school, help them get out of their heads and be kids. Have fun, play a game that does not connect to a D1 scholarship or pro-contract.

10. Teach your kids who they are. Help them understand their identity. If they have a solid understanding of who they are internally, they will be much less likely to look to others to tell them who they are when they offer to them to be somebody they are not.

Homework

When I was a kid in school, I did not think that I could hate homework more than I did while in school. But then I became a parent. And my hate for homework grew to a new level. And to top it all off, I am not even sure how effective homework even is! It is terrible training for life. Go to work all day, then come home and do more work? I know that many of us do this, but should we? Being able to leave work at work and be present at home is a huge milestone for many. I get it; if you own your own business, you are never really off, but separating home life from work life is valuable. And homework does not teach that. And don't get me started on "flipped classrooms". I know some teachers do this well, but some just assign videos to watch at home to teach the kids, then they go to class and do the homework. So the teacher basically can just phone it in and not have to teach. No wonder people are flocking to school options other than public schools!

If you can't tell, I really hate homework. I typically ask teachers at the "meet the teacher" events how much I have to pay for there to just be no homework. Send me the link to the app of choice, and I will deposit the money. It is worth it to just not have to do it.

But how do autism, ADHD, adolescence and being an a-hole shine with homework? Let's investigate.

Autism

In elementary school, my son came home with a worksheet assigned for homework. Knowing he had one-on-one help at school and seeing the worksheet was partially completed, I assumed an adult had helped him finish part of it, and he had the rest for homework. It was a newer style of math that I had not been familiar with. My wife, who was an elementary teacher at the same school my son was at, was at some event, so it was all up to me to help. No problem, I was good at math, and this is third-grade math, so how hard can it be? Since I did not have a textbook and had not been in class to get the instructions, I thought I would just go over the 3 or 4 problems he had worked out with his teacher to familiarize myself with the content. And this is where it got off track. I could not figure it out. The answers did not match the questions. The logic from problem 1 did not translate to 2, but kinda workout on 3. Before long I broke out graph paper, had to find batteries for my TI-82, and I was about to factor in imaginary numbers when I realized this was THIRD GRADE math! So I go to social media for some help. I posted the pic of the problem, and one of his teachers responded, and he later confirmed their response. He had worked on this all by himself. He read the problem, and then thought of a number that he liked, and put that number down. There was absolutely no logic to anything that he did.

In later grades, we eventually worked into my son's IEP that he would not have homework. He is several grade levels behind and is on an alternative diploma track. I say this just so you know: no homework has the potential to exist! But depending on the brand of autism you are experiencing, homework could be a strong suit for a kid with autism. If it is something they know how to do, they can sometimes get really excited about doing homework. So much so that they neglect opportunities to engage socially with others. Homework can provide an escape from the complications of confusing social interactions. They earn great grades on homework assignments, but they might forgo important life lessons they could learn by interacting with family and friends.

But if homework is not as easy to understand, it can get very frustrating. As answers are less black and white, trying to comprehend the gray can be very hard for kids on the autism spectrum. And if they are frustrated with homework, they are very unlikely to approach you calmly and explain that homework is hard and they need help. Instead, you can expect any number of behaviors to manifest that are a representation of the anger, frustration, and fear they are experiencing. Things like yelling at the dog, kicking the wall, intense stemming behaviors, or maybe just running away and eloping. (Have I told you how much I hate homework?)

One thing I have had to learn with autism is that what is being presented to me is rarely what it is. Meaning, there is usually a cause to a reaction that is happening, and that cause is rarely directly or logically (as I define logic) connected to the actual behavior being presented. And given that language processing is often an issue with autism, there is no talking it out and having someone just tell you what the issue is. Often, they don't even know. This is not the "I don't know" of typical adolescence; they really don't know why they are so angry, sad, or afraid. They might not even be able to name the emotions. They are just reacting to the emotion and are expressing what they are experiencing, but still don't know why they are experiencing it.

As much as I get frustrated at this, when I stop to think how this must feel to be him, it helps me muster up some empathy. I can't imagine what it might feel like to just have an influx of emotions with no reason they are there. And if I don't know where they are coming from, how am I supposed to process them? I would likely do the same thing that my son does.

ADHD

Let's see if I can explain the ADHD homework perspective by offering you insight into a potential internal monologue of somebody with ADHD.

> I am going to do my homework. I can't remember what classes assigned what homework, but hopefully it will come to me when I get started. So let's start with math…ding…but I have to answer this text first. No way, they said what online? I have to go check this out online and comment…how does somebody to get a cat to do that; I have got to tell my cat friends this in our text thread…yes; I am going to comment, just give me a moment. "Dinner is ready". Who said that? I don't have time to eat. I have too much homework. Besides, I already had a bag of chips when I got home because my meds wore off and I was starving. "I'm not hungry! I have too much homework to go to dinner!"
>
> Homework. I gotta do that. OK, math…where is my math folder. I can't find my math folder. I must have left it in the kitchen when I got the chips. I will go check, but I need to use the bathroom first. Oh no, I have a zit. I need to wash my face to get that addressed ASAP.
>
> As I get to the kitchen to look for my math folder, Mom says, "Why is there water running in your bathroom?" I forgot to turn it off after I washed my face. "And why is your face wet?" I forgot to dry my face.
>
> "I dunno, Mom, have you seen my math folder?"
>
> "It's not here at the dinner table where you should be!"
>
> "AGHGHG, I HAVE HOMEWORK, MOM. I TOLD YOU, I AM NOT HUNGRY! I CAN'T FIND MY MATH FOLDER!"

Mom, walking to my room, "You mean this math folder open on your desk?" That's right, I got it out then somebody distracted me with a text. A TEXT, I have to respond to that post online, but I still have to use the bathroom! And now I am hungry. Why didn't Mom make dinner?

All the above might sound extreme, and hopefully it is, but this is just a sample of what could be the struggle related to focusing in the afternoon, especially if you have had to hold it all in all day at school. You have spent all your focus at school, and there is just not any left to give at home. And if medications are involved, they have likely worn off right about the time you get home from school.

Meds wearing off can have a few items associated with them. One is hunger. Many ADHD meds (stimulants) have a side effect of suppressing appetite. So when meds wear off, you are starving. And because of poor impulse control, you will eat whatever is in front of you. No matter who is actively fixing what for dinner. You need food, and you need it now. A second side effect can be an emotional crash. Coming off these meds can bring about agitation, anger, or maybe even rage. It can be short-lived, but it is long enough to ruin an evening for the person coming off the meds, and also for the people having to experience it. If this is you, talk with your doctor, as there are some options to mitigate this. But know that it is real, and that your kid likely has little control over it.

But homework and ADHD rarely go well together. It is kind of like peanut butter and scrambled eggs. They just don't mix! It will be a struggle for kids with ADHD to be successful with homework. Homework is hard because of home distractions like phones, TVs, siblings, pets, neighbors, and the fan that makes noise when turned on.

Adolescence

Developmental levels and how much an adolescent cares are factors in homework, in similar ways they are in school. If you don't understand the assignment in class, you are likely not going to understand it at home. And you can't ask your parents, they are idiots. But I want to discuss a different aspect here as we talk about homework, and that is the schedule.

The day of an adolescent is only half over when school ends. Not only are teachers assigning more and more homework as they need to keep pace with state standards that they just don't have time to cover in class, but the number of after-school activities is just not sustainable. Sure, we have always had sports, but even with sports, when I was a kid, it was pretty much just a school team. But now, if you want to get any type of hope of playing in college, you need to be on a club team that travels all over the place. And in order to gain an edge, you likely need a personal trainer and regular gym time, and also a skills-based trainer (e.g., hitting/pitching coach), a nutrition consult, plus a social media presence just for your sports career. Baseball, football, swimming, lacrosse, cheerleading, gymnastics, golf, tennis, you name it…it is like a full-time job. It is not a fun game/activity to do with friends. If you are not fully engaged by the time you get to high school, realistically you are not going to the next level.

And if sports are not your thing, don't think you are off the hook. No matter what the interest is, there are a plethora of offerings to enhance your skills and prepare you for the future. Band is more like a lifestyle. But no program on a high school campus will receive more college scholarships than the band. Now, you are likely not getting a signing bonus that can buy momma a house to play tuba professionally, but you can get a pretty good scholarship and get out of college debt-free! But it takes work in middle and high school to stand out.

And these are just school/scholarship activities. Not to mention the things that you might do because you just want to do them. Things like church or other activities for your own personal growth that may be very important to you from a life development perspective. But they all take time.

Any interest you have can connect you to an after (or before) school activity. And that activity (or more likely activities) will require time. Time to practice, time to plan, time to rehearse, time to learn, time to attend, time to gather...time. And what also takes time? Homework. And somewhere, something has to give. Because you only have so much time. And you also need money, so somewhere in all of this you have to factor in trying to get a job, which also takes...you got it, time.

Learning to prioritize a schedule is a valuable life skill. Unfortunately, our adolescents are busier than we are as adults. (Except we have to take them to all of their activities and attend all their games/performances/competitions/meets/matches/etc.). Most adolescents need a personal assistant. Someone to schedule their meetings, fence their calls, pick up their dry cleaning, schedule lunches, and help reinforce their boundaries. But unless that is you, their parent, this is likely not happening. It is a LOT to manage. Since most of these activities are scheduled from the end of school until about 7-8 PM, homework, by default, doesn't start until late in the evening when they are exhausted, hungry, and done for the day. And I get it. I would be exhausted too. My kids' school starts at 7:20 AM. So we are waking up around 5:45 AM to catch buses. So bedtimes, to get something close to the amount of sleep needed for an adolescent, are in the ballpark of 8 PM on school nights. And unfortunately, we are not even getting home until after 8 PM some nights.

When I was a kid, there were some unspoken rules related to certain days being protected. In the South, you did not have homework or late (if any) practices on Wednesday nights, as there was a general expectation that people went to church on Wednesday nights. And there was never anything planned on a Sunday. Those were literally sacred days. But as we mentioned, with all the things going into schedules, something had to give. So before long, there were no breaks for things that might be family time, or just quiet time. There is always something to do. And even when there is no activity planned, there is always something that needs to be practiced, exercised, and/or refined. It really is a giant ball of stress and pressure that we place on adolescents, and then we wonder why they have epidemic levels of anxiety and depression. They lack life experience and developed brains to handle schedules that rival that of a Fortune 500 CEO, and we wonder why they cannot keep up!

A-Hole

I think that COVID may have impacted kids and homework more than we know. At the time of writing this, kids in high school all experienced the shutdown of COVID. Everything shut down. All the things that we said were so important suddenly were not. And for some kids, even after the world started back up, I don't think they ever turned back on. If school was so important, why did they tell us to stay home and more or less pass us whether or not we knew the content, as long as we could figure out how to make the mouse move every 15 minutes? As adults, we know how much our kids got behind during those times. Teachers are still dealing with the fallout of kids being behind grade level several years after COVID. But for some, COVID just basically said nothing really matters. So why bust my tail to do homework? Why spend a lot of energy on basically anything? It can all just get shut down. I don't think this is everybody, but I think it messed with the minds of more kids than we might think.

I think that this is part of the sourcing of the homework a-hole. They just don't see why it is so important. So they just don't do it. There are some in this homework a-hole camp who have completely mastered the content, perhaps even better than the teacher, and just see no point in spending the next 2 hours of their life proving what they already know. The other end of this spectrum also exists. They did not know what was going on is class, and it is not like they were magically enlightened on the bus ride home. So spending 2 hours doing it wrong just to get a poor grade and feel worse about themselves seems pointless and even more stupid. So they just don't do it.

Others may have just reached a breaking point. There is only so much homework that one can take before they unionize and revolt. They said something about that in History class…taxation without representation…tea was spilt, revolutions started, truths were held self-evident, and we deserve life, liberty, and no homework! Or something like that. And trust me, as a graduate of the International Baccalaureate program who did 5-6 hours of homework a night, there comes a point where enough is enough.

But trying to explain how refusing to do homework is going to tank your grade and limit your future career options is difficult to do with an a-hole, because they likely just don't care. Maybe they have a reason not to care, and maybe it is a good reason, but they just don't care. Maybe not caring is less painful than caring and failing. Maybe other trauma in their life demands so much care in order to survive that they have no care left for homework, but the theme remains consistent: they simply don't care.

Suggestions

1. Empathize. Listen to how your kids feel and try to understand their perspective. Share with them your thoughts, feelings, and perspectives. And if you really loved homework in school, talk about how you have no friends now and are a miserable person and how you want better for your kids!:-)

2. Talk with their teachers. Get an idea of how much time the teacher expects it to take to complete homework, and share how much is actually being spent on homework. Find out what to do if there is a discrepancy.

3. Budget time like you would budget money. Or to say it a different way, have a schedule. I like the budgeting concept because it requires you to set aside time in advance. And if you get done early, it is like you can save time to invest into something else. But you have to pay your bills before you go on a spending spree. (Or at least you should, but that is another topic). This also helps when it comes time to grant requests for extra things. If an activity is going to eat into homework time, having a plan of how to recoup that time is part of the decision-making process.

4. Limit distractions during homework time. Be intentional about setting up distraction-free zones for homework. TVs or any other sound or light-making devices are off. There is nothing interesting to look at (so no big windows watching everybody outside).

5. If distractions are necessary (I know this contradicts the above, so take what works for you), make sure the fidget devices are available so students can use them during homework.

6. Let kids fail. Homework is not the end of the world, nor are grades. Helping your kid learn the importance of homework by letting them get a poor grade and miss out on things can be a great life lesson. One missed homework assignment does not make the difference between poverty and wealth. But learning to be consistent and take responsibility for actions is a great life lesson. We can sometimes learn that lesson only through logical consequences.

7. Get your kid some help. If you can do it, great. Bond with your kid and do it together. If you can't, hire a tutor or do some internet searches for videos. Encourage your kid to reach out to others in class to get some help. After all, we nerds need friends too!

8. Celebrate successes. If your kid completes a project or gets a good grade on a homework assignment, make a big deal out of it. Do something randomly awesome for them to celebrate.

9. Teach kids how to record their assignments. Designate a single spot to record all homework assignments. And help them learn how to estimate how much time it will take them to complete it. Maybe you start with the hardest, maybe you start with the easiest. Maybe it is the longest; maybe it is the shortest. Help them learn what works best for them.

10. Take breaks. People need breaks, and brains need breaks. Learn what the optimal rhythm is. Maybe it is 10 minutes of work, 1 minute of break; maybe it is 30 minutes working, 5 minutes breaking. Do some tests and figure out how to be most productive. This is a great life skill.

Bedtime

Preparing to go to sleep, prepping to end the day, and possibly starting the next day well is something we all do. But for an adolescent on the autism spectrum with ADHD, that is not as easy as it sounds. Sleep is valuable, but learning to prepare for it and how to invite it can be a challenge for anybody, and even more so for those who have some struggles.

Autism

Having a bedtime and bedtime routines are great. And for some on the spectrum, this is not a decision; it is just a way of life. It is not just easy to do; it is hard not to do it. But there are some things that autism can bring to the table that can make it very difficult to go to bed. Let's examine a few.

Overstimulation can take a wrecking ball to bedtime. And please note, this does not have to be something that all would agree is overstimulating; it is anything that is overstimulating to the person on the spectrum. You may not know what caused it, but something pressed the wrong button and now there is just no calming down from it. This might lead to increased stimming, or it could result in a range of emotions from anger to sorrow, or even joy. And unfortunately, none of this helps a person calm down enough to go to sleep.

Perseveration can also wreak havoc on going to bed. If we have not discussed it, or if you have just skipped to this section, this is that feature of autism to just overly focus on one thing. There are elements of it with ADHD as it relates to hyperfocus, but this is different with autism because it is not something that requires or engages all your focus, but something tiny you give all of your focus to. This perseveration becomes overstimulating on its own because releasing it is impossible. We have all experienced this on some level when we just cannot get a thought out of our head. The earworm of a song that just won't leave us alone. Most of us can change the subject and move on, but not so much with autism. It just does not leave; it takes over your mind. While this can happen at any time of the day, when it happens at bedtime, it can mess up sleep for tonight and behavior tomorrow.

Things unfinished can also rear their heads at bedtime. Perhaps a puzzle piece MIA, and it was the last piece to finish the puzzle you suggested doing to help calm the mind instead of screen time. Maybe screen time cut off before the level was complete, or the show they were watching ended in a cliffhanger and did not resolve. Or, a favorite toy went missing and isn't where it should be before bedtime. Whatever the stimulus, something is out of place, and you or your child will probably not go to bed until someone finds it or fixes the situation.

ADHD

For those with ADHD, if there is any task that needs to be completed, doing this at the last minute provides a bit of a rush, and if we are being honest, you will like do your best work with the aid of that rush. Sure, you have had all week to complete the homework assignment that is due at midnight, but you don't start it until 10:30 pm the night it is due. Not that you are tempting fate by waiting so late, it is more like it was just unnecessary to work on it earlier. But now you are in crisis mode. Those with ADHD work much better with this type of pressure on them. The stakes increase, and you must meet a deadline. Who cares that you were supposed to be in bed at 9? You are in the zone and you will flunk out of school if this project that should have taken all week is not done in the next 2 hours! Sleep? Sleep is for the weak. It really is a kind of high that those with ADHD feel when they get into this mode. It is a way of forcing oneself into hyperfocus. And once you have achieved hyperfocus, it is like the runner's high that I have never experienced but people keep telling me about. You just feel invincible. Unfortunately, you are also not sleeping and getting the rest that is necessary for the next day to go well. But that is not your problem now. That is future you's problem.

Self-induced hyperfocus aside, for many with ADHD, you are just not paying attention to the time. The term time blind applies here. You do not know what time it is, or how long it will take you to accomplish certain tasks. So you just don't know that it is 5 minutes before bedtime and you have not begun the routines that are necessary for bed (shower, pajamas, brush teeth, wash face, prep for tomorrow, etc.) that usually take 30 minutes. And you may or may not have been doing anything important leading up to this. You just got distracted. You really want to go to bed on time, and may even agree wholeheartedly with the need for sleep, but you just lost focus.

And for those on medications for ADHD, there is an added component. Not only do you not have the benefit of your medications to help you focus, sometimes coming off of those meds can be a struggle. There can be an emotional letdown that can lead to anger/agitation, but as mentioned earlier, many of these meds suppress your appetite. So late in the day, this is the first time you are actually hungry, and you can't just go to bed because you are starving! And your lack of impulse control does not allow you to wait for a healthy snack, so you eat anything that you can find available. Who cares about the caffeine in that thing that will later keep you awake? After all, you take stimulants all day long!

Adolescence

Adolescents are at one of two extremes with sleep and bedtimes. Either they never sleep and are up all night, or they sleep all the time. Let's start with the latter. It is pretty common for adolescents and adults to have really poor sleep habits. And when you get out of routines of sleep, you might get home from school exhausted and decide to take a nap. And while you do not intend to do so, you sleep for 5 hours. You wake up feeling unrested, and you could have used those 5 hours for homework, especially with assignments due tomorrow. So you just stay up and complete it. You finally get it done at like 3:30 AM and decide to go to bed. But you are hungry, so you go for a snack. By the time you eat that and get ready for bed, it is 4 AM. The alarm goes off at 6 AM for school, so that is a solid 2 hours of sleep. You wake up after considerable prompting (and that is saying nicely) from your parents, and go to school. You are tired all day, nodding off in class, and barely making it home. Now you are tired, so you decide to take a nap...and the cycle repeats. You eventually lose the ability to go to sleep at normal times as your body is acclimating to a new schedule. UNTIL...the weekend comes and you are ready to go off with friends and somehow you can magically stay away all night to hang out with friends. Energy drinks may or may not be artificially propping you up. You get home Saturday afternoon and crash until Sunday night. No joke, you sleep for like 17 hours. But you wake up refreshed at 5 PM on Sunday, with homework to do, which you complete at 3:30 AM, and the cycle repeats.

Perhaps you are reading this as an adult and thinking, wait, that is still happening to me. Sleep is a major element of most mental health conditions. How you can fall asleep, how well you can stay asleep, and how refreshed you feel after sleeping are major diagnostic elements of most mental health issues. Some individuals unfortunately learn and reinforce these poor habits when they are adolescents.

Sometimes, you simply cannot avoid it. If you are involved in after-school activities and are taking intense classes with lots of homework, something has to give. And sleep is all too easy to give up. Never mind that your body is going through massive changes and desperately needs sleep to stay healthy, you must attend practice and you have to turn in this assignment.

The other extreme is just not sleeping and not being tired. For some going through adolescence, the energy level is great. You have all of this excess energy and you are just not tired. So you are staying up super late, getting up super early, and are not tired or groggy. While this might seem like a powerful gift, your body still needs rest. For many who are doing this, they eventually need a crash day where they sleep for most of the day or weekend to reset. While it is not a healthy routine, we certainly see this celebrated. We are told how very successful people wake up at 4 AM, go all day like the Energizer Bunny, and then go to bed at midnight to start it all over again. It is as if we are celebrating this new species of human that only needs 4 hours of sleep. And we also have normalized the need to be productive for 20 hours a day in order to be successful! After all, if you want to get into an excellent school, not only do you have to take advanced classes, but you also have to be a star on a varsity sport and have thousands of hours of community service. And if you can start a business in your spare time and be a viral influencer, you may have a chance!

A-Hole

We should know by now that the a-hole just does not care. This can be true when the a-hole is hungry at 2 AM and makes a gourmet meal in the kitchen. There is really no thought to sounding like the Swedish Chef from the Muppets, as they open and close every single cabinet door, leaving some open, grab every pot and pan from the cabinet, and then bang, scratch, and whisk with all their might. Oh, and they forgot they need to use the blender! And then at 2:45, when their dish is complete, they walk off to their room with the kitchen looking like a war zone, making breakfast preparations all but impossible for whoever comes after them. This is one expression of the a-hole at bedtime, but there are many others.

Perhaps they know that going to bed is important for you, so they intentionally don't go to bed and make as much noise as possible just to tick you off and keep you awake. Or, they wait until you go to bed, then sneak up or out to do the things they know you don't approve of. It becomes really sad as they do not realize how much they are destroying themselves. In their efforts to tick you off, they are harming themselves. And while there is a natural tendency to push boundaries in adolescence to establish their own independence, the a-hole seeks their independence at the expense of others.

And if we are being honest with ourselves, society celebrates this. We talk about this as being trendsetters. These are the ones who push through and past the boundaries that society has set, and they set new standards, explore new territories, push the laws of nature to make new inventions. We love the trendsetters, the boundary breakers. But trying to help your adolescent be a healthy human who is not afraid to challenge the norm to be successful, while not being an a-hole, can be a challenge. After all, what CEO, what rock or movie star, what majorly successful person is not an a-hole? How much of an a-hole is just the right amount to be successful, and how much is too much so that you wind up in prison? That margin is very small.

Suggestions

1. Have bedtimes and well-established routines. Set reminders well before those bedtimes to announce that bedtime is nearing.

2. Promote healthy sleep hygiene. This is not specific to bedtime, but is a way of life. (It has its own section coming up, so keep reading.) Adolescents need sleep, and lots of it.

Protecting the time for sleep to happen may mean saying no to other great things. Just because an activity might end in time to allow one to be home in time for bedtime, how stimulating is that activity? Will there be time to decompress?

3. Model healthy sleep habits. Your kids will follow what you do much more than they will follow what you say. And while you may need less sleep than they do, you can still model healthy habits.

4. Have healthy snacks available in case the med crash or the munchies hit close to bedtime. Make those sleep healthy snacks. No caffeine or chocolate, or things with a great deal of sugar in them. Unhealthy snacks like these will provide spurts of energy that will make it harder to sleep.

5. Turn the lights down as you get close to bedtime. Having a room that is darker with dim or soft lighting will help the brain realize it is time to shut down.

6. Limit screen time or stimulating activities before bed. Make it a habit to turn off screens about an hour before bed. This gives time for the brain to decompress and makes space for nightly routines.

7. Don't bring up controversial or involved topics right before bed. This may be your only time to discuss things with your kids, but starting a conversation about grades, friends, activities, etc. can start off a series of thoughts that may make it hard to go to bed. Use this time to speak affirmations to your kids. Speak life into them. Share your love and appreciation. Model gratitude.

8. This will sound like a contradiction to the above, but sometimes your kid may need to process something before they can sleep. The difference here is that they are bringing up the controversial topic, not you. If it is really heavy on

their mind, they could use the help of a trusted adult to process it and allow them to sleep. And don't be upset if you are not that trusted adult. It may be a grandparent, an uncle, a youth pastor, or a really mature friend that they just need to talk to. Learn the difference between just wanting to stay up to chat versus needing to work through something heavy. Be intentional about encouraging healthy relationships with other healthy adults who can say the same thing you would say and are just not you!

9. When exceptions happen and routines need to be interrupted, don't just take time away from sleep. Be sure you allow time for sleep in the schedule. Meaning, if you need to stay up 3 hours later, make it okay to sleep in for 3 hours the next day. I get that life may not make this possible, but sleep is important. Don't get into the habit of teaching it is okay to rob it.

10. Check in with your kid in the morning. Teach them how to rate their sleep from the night before. Did they get up at all? Do they feel rested? How long did it take them to fall asleep? Were they lying in bed awake for several hours in the night after falling asleep? Learning to measure the quality of sleep will help you help them. If there are patterns, you may need to make other adjustments to routines, or you may need to talk with a professional.

Part III

Taking Care of Me, While Taking Care of Autism, ADHD, Adolescence, and A-holes.

We have talked a good bit about the differences in how each "A" can impact any situation. The idea behind this is that knowing which "A" you are dealing with will give you a chance to best address the need and get the desired outcome. This last section will not focus on the "A's" but is going to focus on you, the caregiver/parent/guardian. Providing care at this level of difficulty takes a toll on a person. Caring for someone with specialized needs is draining emotionally, physically, mentally, spiritually, relationally, and financially. Caring for yourself allows you to better care for your kids. When you are healthy, rested, at peace with self and others, you are a better parent and a better person. But who has time to take care of themselves when there are so many needs that others have? I know, I get it, that struggle is real. So let's talk through a few areas where we can easily set things aside. You may hear this a lot, but taking time for self is not selfish

Rest

You are not a machine. You need downtime. Even machines need downtime for maintenance. When we talk about rest, I don't just mean sleep. Sleep is a part of it, and we will get to that, but it is only a part. Rest can also mean the activities you do that replenish you. Sometimes that is things you do all by yourself, and other times that means activities you do with friends. I encourage you to take an inventory of what activities add energy to you and what activities take it away. Are you a people person, or do people drain you? Do you need to build something, or does sitting down with a good book do it for you? Knowing you and what refills you is huge. If you need help to figure this out, ask a spouse/partner/friend. They can probably tell you pretty quickly. If those people are not present in your life or you just don't feel comfortable asking (especially if you already know the answer and you don't want to hear it from one of them:-)), reach out to a counselor. It is totally worth the investment in you to figure this out. Self-care is not selfish!

Here are a few questions to ask yourself, your friend, or have your counselor work through with you.

- What makes me feel most alive?

- What activity drains me the most?

- What activity do I never dread doing?

- What activity to I dread doing but am later glad I did?

- If I had free time and extra money, what would I do?

- What have I not done in a long time that I miss?

- Who do I most want to hang out with and why?

- If I were the best and healthiest version of myself, I would probably…?

- What do I envy about others?

- What do I have the hardest time saying "no" or "yes" to?

If you take a few minutes to answer these questions, I hope you will get a better picture of what might provide you the fuel to replenish yourself. For me, I need to be alone, preferably out in nature somewhere. This has always been my happy place. When I watch the movie Castaway, it shocks me why you would ever leave that place! It seemed like pure paradise. I like people and have professionally been involved in careers that help people, thus making me interact with people. I enjoy it, but I am exhausted after an event that involves numerous people. My wife is just the opposite. Walking in the woods is pure torture for her. If she is quiet for long periods of time, she is sick, angry, or both. And in all honesty, this was a struggle for us early in our relationship. After we came home from a gathering of people, she had energy and wanted to talk and have fun, while I felt drained. It was hard for us to understand each other and not take it personally when I was just "talked out" after an event that I had to be "on" for. Because we have taken the time to understand ourselves and each other, when we have a people event, she knows I need to decompress and she probably needs to go call her friends to talk. She has been encouraging of me taking personal time away as we have progressed down our journey because she can see I need it, and she sees the benefits for me (and herself), even when I don't see it for myself.

I also enjoy activities where I have control. So much of my world as a parent of a special needs child is out of my control. In my career, where I am helping people, I can offer advice and guidance, but it is totally up to another person with free will to choose to implement this. I am not in control. So I like activities where I can be in control. Woodworking is a hobby that allows this for me. Tech at my church also scratches this itch. As complicated as an audio console can be, it will do just exactly what I tell it to do. And if something goes wrong, it is because I told it to do something wrong and it did it. It is very restoring for me. I am also in the back and in the dark, and if I am doing my job right, nobody knows I am there. It is perfect for me. My wife, on the other hand, loves to be on stage and sing and interact with others on stage and the audience. It is life-giving for her.

I mention these, particularly the differences that we have, to highlight that just because it works for you does not mean it is going to work for others in your life. There are times I need to sacrifice and be a people person for my wife, and support her as she is the bell and/or belle of the ball. There are other times when she needs to walk quietly with me in the woods and just listen to the birds chirp. And both of us need to sacrifice for each other and both offer and receive the gift being given in order for a relationship to work. Not only can this be true if you are in a relationship, but can also apply with the person you are caring for. What replenishes you may not replenish them. Take the time to learn what works for you and for them, and make this rest a part of your routine. It is much better to intentionally seek out rest than to burn out and have it forced upon you. Sometimes, if you wait too long, the rest that is forced on you involves a bright orange or stripped jumpsuit or a padded room!

Sleep Hygiene

While part of rest is what you do, sleep is another aspect of rest. It is a big part of getting the resources you need to function. If you have absolutely no problem with sleeping and feel rested each morning, I implore you to stop what you are doing and offer praise and thanks to your God for this gift you have been given. You are in a small minority on the planet. Struggles with sleep are all too common, and much of that has to do with poor sleep hygiene. We will share information focused on you as the caregiver, but the same principles will apply to the person you are caring for. Sleep hygiene is a way of life, not just something you do at bedtime. So I will begin this discussion with the moment you wake up, and then walk through the day. Please note, if you are having difficulty with sleep, doing these things one day will not immediately guarantee you will have awesome sleep. Just like going to the gym one day will not make you look like a bodybuilder. This is about consistency and living a healthy life. If what I am about to describe seems completely overwhelming to you, then start by picking one thing we are going to talk about and try to apply that to your life. Then maybe add others as you go along. It is also not a bad idea to discuss this with a health professional if you are really struggling in this area.

Wake Up

I know it sounds weird to start the discussion with sleep hygiene at the moment you wake up, but hopefully by the end of this you will see the importance. With waking up, try to wake up at roughly the same time each day. I am not saying you have to wake up when the sun comes up, but whatever time you are going to wake up, wake up at that same time each day. For those who work a more traditional 9-5 job, on the weekends, resist the urge to sleep in all day long. Maybe give yourself an extra 30 minutes, but try to keep the same schedule. If you are working shift work where you are on nights part of the week and then on days, this is extremely challenging for sleep health. So whatever rhythm you get into for that transition from days to nights, keep it consistent. A shift-dependent schedule may mean some of your wake up times may not be the same time each day, but might be based on the number of hours you sleep, but that is a much more complicated discussion that is worth having with someone with some experience in this area, and is beyond the scope of this work, but the point is, be consistent with what time you get up. No matter how complicated your schedule is, do your best to build in some consistency.

Learn to evaluate your previous night's sleep. Even better if you can write it down. There is a good deal of wearable tech these days that will tell you what level of sleep you had, but if you can make evaluating your sleep a regular part of your wake up routine, it will provide you with valuable information to adjust your routines or to provide to a health professional if you need to have other interventions to assist your sleep.

Here are a few items to help you in considering how to evaluate your sleep. A few things that don't have obvious answers may require you to assign a 0-10 scale to (0 = worst ever, 10 = best ever):

- How rested do I feel? (0-10)

- What time did I go to bed?

- How long did it take to fall asleep (this can be a time or a 0-10)

- Did I stay asleep once I fell asleep?

- How many times did I get up last night?

- Did I wake up and could not go back to sleep?

- If I had trouble with sleep, was there an external factor preventing this (partner sick, outside construction, AC broken, etc.)

Once you get up, make it bright. Light is a big part of helping our bodies know when it is time to wake up, and the absence of light, as we will discuss in a minute, will cue your body it is time to go to sleep. There is this enormous ball in the sky that is a global cue that we should be awake. As it goes away later in the day, it is our cue that it is time to go to sleep. In parts of the world where this does not happen (extreme north and south) where it will be light for 23 hours a day parts of the year and dark 23 hours a day for other parts of the year, this is a huge problem, as it really messes people's sleep cycles up, causing all kinds of problems. But for those of us not in those extremes, making your morning bright could involve opening up a curtain, but if you beat the enormous ball of fire up, then you may need to have lamps on. This light cues your brain that it is time to wake up and be active.

Have good and consistent morning routines. By the time you get done with this section, you may tire of hearing me talk about routines, but these are really important to healthy sleep hygiene. And in all honestly, the more difficulties you are having with sleep, the more you will need the routines. If you are not having difficulties with sleeping, either you already have great routines and don't realize it, or you are just a freak of nature and don't need them. If this is you, you are probably not reading this book, and if so, are only reading this chapter to see how the rest of us struggle. But either way, congratulations on being superhuman! But for the rest of us, we need some structure on how we wake up so we can also provide some structure in how we sleep.

Morning routines can be very simple. You pee (let's be honest, everybody does this) and then things like brushing teeth, taking medications, washing your face, changing clothes (even if this is just changing a shirt if you are going to lounge around the house on a day off) can be a huge part of a morning routine that cues your brain that it is time to boot up and get started for the day.

Breakfast

Literally, this word, "breakfast" or "break" "fast" is exactly what you are doing. You have fasted for several hours while sleeping, so you need to break that fast, which is where we get the word breakfast. I get it, some people are not big eaters in the morning. And if you are not having difficulties with sleep, this may not be you. But if you are having trouble with sleep, eat something and eat it consistently after you wake up. There are a few benefits to this. First, it wakes up parts of your body that were previously dormant. Parts like your digestive system and your vagal nervous system become active when you put food in your mouth and swallow. It forces your body to wake up to process the food.

While any food will work to start your wake-up process, picking the right food will better propel you throughout your day. For example, foods with a bunch of sugar will jumpstart your system, but will leave you empty and drained in a short time when your body has burned through all of this. So foods that will give better fuel for the long run, like protein, more complex sugars like you would find in fruits, and a few carbs (bread or potatoes) will help give you the fuel you need to propel you through your morning. If you are a coffee person, now is the time to consume caffeine. We will talk in a bit about the caffeine cutoff time.

This is also a good time to move your body. Maybe you do this before breakfast, maybe you do it after, and if you are really talented and an overachiever, you might do them both at the same time. If you want to do a full exercise routine, that is great, but at this point in the game, go for a quick walk. Getting your body moving in the morning helps train and condition your brain that it is time to wake up.

And while we are at it, make your bed. Nobody is going to do a room inspection, but a made bed is less inviting to re-enter (more to come on this). Plus, no matter how bad your day goes, when it is time to end it, a made bed is a reminder that you started the day off right.

Midday

This one is key. No matter how tired you are, don't go back to bed. Bed is for sleeping and another word that starts with "s" but this is not that type of book. If you got back to bed, you are not doing yourself any favors. You are training your brain to sleep during the day and not so much at night. So, as best as you can, keep to your plans, even if you are tired. Now there are obviously limits here. If you are falling asleep, you should likely not be operating a vehicle or heavy equipment. But as best as you can, be active during the midday. No naps is the standard. But if you have to nap during a transition, only 20 minutes, and absolutely no naps after 3 PM. And nap somewhere other than bed.

By noon, start cutting yourself off from coffee. No caffeine after 4 PM. This gives this drug, that's right, it is a drug, time to get out of your system before you try to sleep. If coffee is a part of your culture and you just have to keep drinking it, switch to decaf after noon. But plan on no coffee after noon, no caffeine after 4 PM.

Midday is the best time to conclude exercise. As we mentioned earlier, exercise can wake you up. It will boost certain neurotransmitters and hormones, most of which are going to wake you up. So you want to have all your exercise done 4-6 hours before you plan to go to bed.

Alcohol also needs to be wrapped up 4-6 hours before bed. While alcohol is a depressant, and will slow your system down and may relax you a bit, it will not help you get to a full and deep sleep. Most who use alcohol to fall asleep find they do not wake up as rested as they would like. Please hear me, I am not the alcohol police. And if you are not struggling with sleep, carry on. But if you got furious at the thought of not drinking alcohol 4-6 hours before bed, it may be time to do some soul searching and talk to a trusted friend or a professional as to how much of a role alcohol plays in your life, and whether it is healthy.

Prepping for Bed

Think of this as 90 minutes before you want to go to bed. Whatever your bedtime is, start this an hour and a half before that time.

As best you can, dim the lights. If the overhead lights are on and bright, turn them off and turn on a lamp. If you can dim lights, do so. Some bulbs these days can even change color temperatures. If so, make them less white (or a lower Kelvin temperature). In much the same way as we want to make it bright in the morning to wake up, we are operating on the inverse here. You want to help your brain understand that it is getting dark and time to shut down for sleep.

One hour (60 minutes) before bed, turn all screens off. This includes TVs, tablets, computers, phones, gaming systems, any screen that will pump light into your face, and also content that will overstimulate your brain. The idea here is not only to get light out of your face, but to let your brain calm down. I get it, this can be hard and depend on our phones. And if sleep is not a problem for you and you can be on your phone right up to bedtime and fall asleep like a baby, then doom-scroll on. But if you are not resting well, put the phone down. Ideally, in another room. And before you say it, just go buy an alarm clock. They are cheap. The costs of not sleeping well are far more expensive than a cheap alarm clock.

So what are you going to do in that 60 minutes of no screen-time? Take a bath or a shower. Our bodies like to be cool to fall asleep. A bath or a shower will naturally lower your body temperature. You may also need to adjust the thermostat a degree or so to make the room cooler. You may find a fan to be helpful here. Taking a bath or shower can also be a great way to just wind down. There are several senses stimulated. Ground yourself by taking a moment to feel and hear the water, smell the soap, and just relax. If while you are in the shower you are just constantly going over the to-do list for the next day, this is probably not going to help. Use that time to relax, stay in the moment, and just calm your mind.

After your shower or bath, your bedtime routine needs to be pretty consistent. Meaning that what you do each night before you go to bed needs to be the same. Whatever that is for you, do it the same way in the same order every night before bed. This might be brushing teeth, taking medications, changing into PJs, applying lotion, etc. Whatever it is, do it the same way every night.

And on your way to bed, if you have not already done so earlier (ideally before your bath so as not to give a free show to the neighbors), close all the curtains and make it as dark and as quiet as possible.

In Bed

As mentioned earlier, you should not go to bed until you are ready to sleep. Don't read in bed, don't play on your phone in bed; do that somewhere else. And by the way, reading something is a great alternative activity for when you turn your screens off. Just don't do that in bed. Bed is for sleeping. So don't get into bed until you are ready to sleep. If bed is the absolutely only piece of furniture you have to sit on, and you have to read or study in bed, do so backwards so that your feet are where your pillows are, and your head is where your feet should be. You want your brain to associate lying down in bed with sleeping.

While in bed, learn to relax your body. Perhaps this is breathing exercises like box breathing. (4 seconds breath in, hold for 4 seconds, breath out for 4 seconds, wait 4 seconds and do it again). Another great exercise to do is to flex and then relax every muscle in your body. Start with your toes, squeeze your toes, then relax them. Next are calves, thighs, butt, stomach, chest, hands, arms, face…squeeze them one at a time for about 2-3 seconds each, then relax them. This will do a few things. First, it forces you to relax your muscles. And by paying attention to your body and the feeling of each muscle flexing then relaxing, it also gets more challenging to let your thoughts race…those same thoughts that are keeping you from falling asleep. Go from toe to head, then head to toe.

If after about 20 minutes of trying to fall asleep you have not fallen asleep, get up. Don't just lie in bed for hours. Go find a really boring book to read and sit somewhere outside of your bed with a dim light and read it. For me, that was a book called Ancient Iraq that my Old Testament Backgrounds class in college assigned me to read. Twenty-seven years have passed, and I still have not finished it because I keep falling asleep while reading it! You may also try journaling. If your thoughts are racing, writing a few notes down will help you clear your mind. When you get tired, go back to bed and try sleeping again.

When you wake up in the morning, the process starts all over again. Evaluate your sleep and make adjustments. Remember, doing this one time is not going to magically fix all sleep problems; it is about consistency. And if you are in a great routine, one night of the unexpected will not derail you for good. You will absorb this because you have a good routine.

Relationships

It is easy for relationships to suffer as you continue down the journey of caring for someone with special needs. Sometimes, it is the busyness of your life that takes away from your relationships. Other times, you just don't want to share what is happening. You didn't want to experience it to begin with, and you certainly don't want to relive it by telling it to somebody else, especially if the person you are going to share it with has no way of understanding what you are saying because they don't live in a special-needs world. They listen, but they don't understand. And the more they try to give advice, the less you want to share!

The reality is we need people. We are designed to connect with others. Infants who do not feel human touch and interactions, fail to thrive. Solitary confinement is a strict punishment in prison. Humans are wired to connect with other humans. Some of us are just harder to connect with than others. This is one reason it can get so frustrating when we share our souls with others, and they just give us pity rather than connection. For some hearing of our struggles, it can sound like you are describing life on a foreign planet. They just don't have a frame of reference. And it is unfortunate that instead of taking the time to just listen and try to understand, they try to fix it, or they just dismiss it because it is too much. If I can vent for a moment, here are a few phrases people intend with love, but I just have a hard time hearing:

"I just don't know how you do it."

"You are a really special person for being able to do all that you do."

"It takes a special person to deal with all of this."

"God will not put more on you than you are able to bear."

"I could never do what you do."

What I would rather hear is:

"Man, your life sucks. I am so sorry."

"I know I can't really do much to help, but I am here for you if you need to talk/scream/cuss."

"When can I come hang out with your person to give you a little bit of a break?"

"What can I take off your plate so you can spend more time doing things only you can do?"

"Clearly God is punishing you for some horrible sin you have committed. If you want to confess, I'm happy to hear it. (then we laugh together)"

Unfortunately, you may need to teach people how to be better friends. And this also sucks. When a person does not know about your world, they may need a guide to teach them how to progress down this path. And on the flip side, you may need to learn to temper yourself and your stories. Being the proverbial "Debbie Downer" in every conversation you enter, will lead to people avoiding you. Not everybody needs to hear all of your woes all the time. You really need to read the room. If you are in the checkout line at the grocery store, it is not a time to go into an intense dialogue about the struggles your child is having with medication. Most of the time when somebody says, "How are you?" they really don't want to know how you are. They are just saying hi. Learning how much to share, and how much not to share, will help you build relationships. There will come a time when someone will ask how you are and they really want to know and you really need to share, but know the difference. It is better to be asked for more details than to over share to someone who couldn't care less. This will be painful for you, and it will be off-putting for them.

You may need to rehearse how to respond to social platitudes when you go into these types of situations. Find something positive to share that is truthful, and make a point to be succinct but positive. As there are opportunities for additional engagement, share as much as the person you are talking to will receive. Learn to pay attention to non-verbals. See when someone is looking uncomfortable and change the subject for them. While this person may not provide you with the connection you need at this point, if you give them an out, they may come back and ask for more. If you burn the bridge just so you can emotionally vomit on someone who is not ready for it, you miss out on future opportunities to connect.

And if you are at the point where you are just one step away from an emotional vomit, we will discuss this in a moment. This is a warning sign that it is time to get some help. But for this section on relationships, there are safe people with whom you can emotionally vomit, but not everybody can receive this.

If you have people who are honest enough to tell you this, ask them what is the first thing they think when they see your name pop up on their phone as a text message or a phone call. You might not like what you hear, but it can help you make some changes to how you present yourself, and may allow you to grow and build better relationships.

If you are married, this is the primary relationship that needs strength, but also one that can be most impacted. While your spouse gets it, as they are living in the same environment as you, they also have a different interpretation of events. They see things you don't, and you see things they don't. You have different upbringings and unique personalities, and most of the time these are opposite of each other. So when you try to solve for problems that exist with the 4 A's, you likely are not going to initially or naturally agree on the best course of action. Failure to check this can lead to a great deal of conflict and division. This difference of opinion can also lead to better and more comprehensive care if you take the time to consider the different perspectives and work together on a solution. But amid the struggle, it's easy to shut someone out or down just to survive.

This book does not aim to be a marriage guide, and if your marriage has already ended in divorce, co-parenting can present a whole new set of issues. But I hope that some of what we have discussed related to the four A's will allow you and your child's other parent (whether or not your spouse) and any additional caregivers who may be involved, to have a few different lenses by which to process what you are observing. Perhaps others can understand situations differently, and learning to listen will allow you to arrive at a better solution. I would encourage you to take the time and spend the money necessary investing into your relationships. Learning things like communication and forgiveness (whether you are married or divorced) can be a tremendous asset for you as you care for someone with special needs. It can dramatically lower the stress in your life and reduce some of the chaos.

Or Is It Me?

Yes, your person can be a challenge, and at any point in time they can be any single or all four of the A's. Amid this complexity and uncertainty, it is good to self-reflect and check in with yourself and check on yourself. How might you be contributing to some of the chaos around you?

What I have found in my life is that it is usually not obvious that I am the problem, or at least not obvious to me. Most of the time, I am worn down one day at a time. From one day to the next, I don't notice the decline or the depletion of resources, but when you measure from one week to the next or one month to the next, you really can see a marked difference.

If you have made it this far, and especially if you just skipped straight here, kudos to you for being willing to consider that you have a role in all of this. Many people easily dismiss that their problems relate to themselves, blaming others instead (this is a classic a-hole response, by the way), but you show a great deal of maturity and health by taking the time to self-reflect.

Here is the plan for this section. I want to point out a few warning signs that could show, if present, that you might be part of the problem. As we walk through these warning signs, if you find an area where you see yourself, it may require a little more on your part to further investigate this area. After we discuss the warning signs, we will focus on some solutions.

Warning Signs

If you are finding one or more of these creeping up in your life, it is a good time to reach out for help. This is not saying you are crazy if you have any of these things; it is saying you are a normal human being with limits. Unfortunately, the job of caring for someone with special needs requires more than what a normal human has to offer. So what I am planning to point out is not something that is a rare occurrence for parents/caregivers of those with special needs; it is pretty common. It is just not talked about as well as it should be.

First, sleep. I know, we just talked about that related to your person. But if you are having difficulty sleeping, either you can't fall asleep, you can't stay asleep, or when you wake up you don't feel rested, this is a warning sign you should pay attention to. If you are following good practices with sleep hygiene and you are still having difficulties, talk to somebody. I suggest starting with your primary care doctor, but you may also need to connect with a therapist or a psychiatrist. You may need a sleep study, you may need to work out some stresses, or you may need medication to assist you. Needing help is not bad. Needing help and not getting it kinda sounds like you may be trending towards a-hole territory:-).

Second, how well are you moving? This could include exercise, but to state it simply, how active are you? If you are lethargic, don't want to get out of bed, don't want to leave the house, and rarely move your body, this is a problem. I am not talking about being a gym-rat, but do you go for a walk? Play a sport? Ride a bike? If you are finding this difficult or painful, it is time to get some help. Maybe join a pickleball league, go to a local park and walk around, find a mall-walker club, do something to get you moving. This is really important for your health.

Third, check your diet. Are you overeating, under-eating, binging certain foods to drown your sorrows? With any of these, I am not talking about something that happens for a day. If you sleep all day because your kid is with somebody else, or you just feel lazy one day, or you pound an entire bag of Oreos, this is not what I am talking about. But if you went to Costco and bought the restaurant pack of Oreos and are eating a sleeve each night, then we are seeing a pattern. If your overall diet is not healthy, or is trending in that direction, then it is a warning sign. This is a time to seek help. You might find this help from a friend, but you might also need a nutritionist or even your physician. Please do not struggle alone.

As a mental health counselor, these first three — sleep, move, and food — are extremely powerful in helping to accurately and quickly diagnose mental health. When any one or more of these are off, it is like a check engine light on a car; additional investigation is usually needed. Rather than just putting a piece of tape over the light, get things checked out. Please hear me, I am not trying to diagnose you, and you may not have or need a diagnosis, but I am encouraging you that if one of these three are off, it is probably not going to resolve itself without some sort of intervention on your behalf.

While these three are a general indicator of health, let's look at a few things that are more specific to being a caregiver of those with special needs.

How much can you put up with? Are you finding yourself more easily irritated and agitated? Do the smallest of things disproportionately set you off? If so, this is a warning sign. To help illustrate this, I use the analogy of a stress cup. There is a certain amount of stress that all of us carry around in our metaphorical stress cup. Once that stress builds up, we need a way of releasing it, or pouring something out of the cup. If we develop healthy routines, this process is pretty easy. We get stress poured into our cups, and we use healthy ways to pour out that stress. So when a little extra stress comes our way, we have room to absorb it healthily. But when stress arrives faster than our ability to release it healthily, or we lose that ability, we carry far more stress than is healthy. So when the cup is almost full, it only takes a small amount of stress for it to spill out. If you overreact to the smallest of stressors, then this is a warning sign your stress cup is too full. For example, if you are at a red light and the person in front of you is taking a few extra seconds to go, and you are screaming at them at the top of your lungs…warning sign. If your kid has lost something, the very thing that you told them to put in a certain spot 2,472 times, and them losing it this time sends you into a seething fit…warning sign. Yes, it is annoying, but if your reaction to it is out of proportion or out of character…warning sign.

Vices

We all need ways to soothe our pain. The pain is real, and we need to cope. This is not a warning sign; this is normal living. But what becomes a warning sign is when you don't just use those things to cope, but you need them to function. When you can't do without them, you plan your day around them, or you avoid activities that would prevent you from being able to use them…this might be a sign to, at the least, have a conversation with somebody.

The speed with which you might want to talk to somebody is related to the degree to which the vice you use can alter you or destroy you. For example, if you are using substances that are illegal and have a chance not just to alter your mood/perception, but can also wind you up incarcerated or dead, talk to somebody sooner rather than later.

I have known people for whom exercise became dangerous. The need to exercise was so intense that it was destroying them. Thankfully, this is not my issue, but going to food can be. Food is not illegal, but it can be destructive and unhealthy if it becomes an unhealthy pattern in your life.

That glass of wine is not bad, but when the glass once or twice a week turns into a glass nightly, or a bottle a night, while you may go to work and complete your tasks, it still may be a good time to talk to somebody.

There are ways to cope that won't destroy you. Taking the time and energy to invest in better ways to process the pain or frustrations you are experiencing is going to be worth it. But please hear me: if you are trying to find something to give you the same feeling as your substance of choice, nothing is going to feel exactly the same. And while it may not work as quickly, a healthier way to cope may keep alive!

Isolation

Isolation can be a challenge. The more problematic the behavior of your person is, the less likely you are to take your person out in public. With all the variables that exist in public, it can just be easier to stay at home. And while that might limit the outbursts and walks of shame you have to experience, it also isolates you. If you don't have somebody to share the burdens you are going through, my heart goes out to you. Keep reading; we offer some options for help. But how do you know you are isolating? Let's start with this one question: When is the last time you had a conversation with another adult? If you took a minute to think, or had to get out a calendar to see…this might be a warning sign. If you get invited out and you have coverage to care for your person, and you just did not want to go because nobody there was going to get you or understand your situation…warning sign. I completely get wanting and valuing alone time. This is me. But when I spend so much time with myself that I don't want to spend it with anybody else, I know I am having a problem where I have swung too far into isolation.

Loss of Hope

Losing hope is major. Along this journey as a parent of someone with special needs, I have had to mourn many losses. When you realize there are some things that your child may never get to experience, and some things you may never get to experience with your child, there is a great deal of loss and grief. But when you lose hope altogether that tomorrow will not be better, this is a warning sign that you need help. And please hear me: there may be a reality that tomorrow will not get much better. I am not trying to tell you to make something up and lie to yourself, but you certainly do not need to go through this journey alone. And if you are losing hope, it is a dangerous place to find yourself.

Thoughts

Check your thoughts. If you are thinking about death, particularly your own death on a somewhat consistent basis, this is not something you should keep to yourself. Now, if you got cut off in traffic and had to slam on the brakes and think, "I almost died!", this is not what I am talking about. But if you are just going about your business and are thinking about death and dying, about your own life ending, or about ending the life of another, this is something you should not keep to yourself. You really should talk to somebody. Most healthy people do not spend time thinking about their death. And if ever those thoughts head towards contemplating how to go about ending your life, this has gone beyond a check engine light. Smoke is coming out of the engine. You should really seek help if those thoughts are starting to trend towards actions.

Reach out to a friend, a pastor, a medical professional, or call 988 to get somebody to talk to. Do that right now. Please do not have these thoughts alone!

Getting Help

Getting help to raise your child with special needs is a must, but this is not the type of help I am talking about. I am talking about getting help for you, the parent or caregiver. When you are evaluating if you are part of the issue, and you need help to determine that, or you have already seen some of these warning signs present in your life and you know you need something more, where do you go? I want to start at the beginning and see if we can work on rebuilding the foundation. If you are finding cracks in the foundation, fixing the roof is great, but if the foundation is not right, problems with continue to exist until you address the deeper issue.

At the foundation, how is your faith? Who or what are you trusting in to make sense of life? Did you have a belief in God and lose it? Is me talking about God right now making you uncomfortable? Here is why I believe this is important. Your belief in how this world came to be and how it works is a major part of developing a worldview. If you have faith in a God that is in charge and in control, who has made humans, even your human who has some special needs, in His image, then by default your child's life has value and worth. This has a vast influence on how much you can endure. Trust me, nothing has challenged my faith, made me question my faith, and just had me argue with God like being a parent of a special needs child. But at the same time, nothing has strengthened my faith more than being a parent of a special needs child. If you have not taken the time to figure out where you are with God, or have not taken time to have a good shouting match with God, I highly encourage you to do so. But please stick around long enough to let Him respond. If you are doing all the talking and refuse to listen…kinda sounds like somebody we have been talking about in this book! If faith is part of your struggle, then reach out to get some spiritual help. Schedule some time with your clergy or a counselor experienced with faith struggles. Find a friend that seems really strong in their faith and at least ask for prayer. If this opens the door to sharing more, then accept the help and get the healing you need.

In addition to a strong faith, you need a friend. Wouldn't it be nice if there were a friend tree somewhere, right next to a money tree, where you could just go pick out a few friends along with some cash whenever you need it? Finding a friend can be hard work. And the longer you are on this journey of parenting a special needs child, the more difficult it becomes to interact naturally with others, as you are not attending games, plays, etc., where people share similar life circumstances. But there are options.

First, check out many advocacy groups. Organizations like CARD (Center for Autism Related Disorders) have local chapters that offer support. Talk to your child's providers (therapists, doctors, psychiatrists) about groups in your community. Some churches do a better job than others of ministering to those with special needs. Seek them out. While your kid might get support in a specialized way, you may also find a community of other parents who are going through a similar journey. My wife and I have been able to get connected with Special Olympics. While our son gets to enjoy the sport and competing, we have found community and support from the coaches and parents of other athletes.

And if all of that sounds overwhelming, consider talking to a therapist. Whatever path you choose to take, you need to let out some of the stress you are carrying around. A therapist is a great way to have somebody to just share with. Even if you have a great community around you, a therapist can be a safe person who will listen to you. They also have a different perspective that can help you process thoughts because they are not so deep in your situation and they can see it differently. They may also have in-roads to community resources you are not aware of. Therapy can be a great place to go to get the strength and courage to go into some of these new spaces to gain additional support and community.

And especially if you are having thought of harming yourself or others, a doctor or therapist needs to be involved. You may also want to call 988 for crisis support if those thoughts are getting more focused, and especially if you are having difficulty dismissing them.

Have a Purpose

Having gone through a few warning signs, let's dig a little deeper into purpose. Please note, if you are not well, take the time to get well. As we will discuss in a bit, this is a necessary step to gaining a purpose.

With the word purpose, I am talking about being able to know why you are doing what you are doing. Amid caring for someone with complex needs who has tendencies to be a jerk, and especially a jerk to you, whether they intend to be a jerk or if it just comes naturally, it's hard to keep going. When you have a reason to keep going, it makes all the difference.

In his book, Man's Search for Meaning, Holocaust survivor Viktor Frankl tells, in painstaking details, the horrors of a Nazi Death Camp, and how some who were strong and healthy did not survive, but others, who seemed to have less physical strength did. What he concluded (and there is no way this can spoil the read) was that those who had a reason to keep going, did. Those who lost hope quickly died.

If you have a reason to keep going, a purpose for providing good care, it makes it easier to stay in the fight. When you lose hope or just lack a purpose, it is so very easy to get burned out, provide poor care, or even head towards your own demise.

What is your win? How will you know if you have succeeded as a parent? For kids that do not have special needs, you have some defined transitions like college, moving out, marriage, or becoming a grandparent. Your role as a parent does not end, but it certainly transitions along the journey.

But with a special needs child, you may not get those easily defined transitions. Graduating from school could mean a lot of extra unsupervised time on your hands. Your person may never leave your care. As they get older, they may require more care. Whatever your situation, what is your purpose? How do you know if you are doing a good job?

I can tell you from personal experience, it can get easy to fall into the trap of comparison. And social media can be very depressing. When you see other kids your child's age navigating life's natural transitions that your child cannot manage, excitement for your friends can mix with sadness as you mourn another loss. My advice is to take a moment to feel the pain. Speak it out loud to somebody close to you. Let it out. If you have not read Boundaries by Cloud and Townsend, I highly recommend it. One boundary law they discuss is the Law of Envy. One question to consider if someone else has something you desire is whether you can legitimately acquire what they have. If you can, set some goals and change some behaviors and get it. If you cannot, mourn the loss and let it go.

How do you mourn the loss? Start out by naming the loss. It helps you define the concern as it allows you to take back some power over the loss when you name it. (Ever notice why we give hurricanes names? Same concept.) Once you name it, feel it. Take a moment to feel the loss. I have some people in my life who will try to argue with me and tell me how good things really are when I am baring my soul about whatever loss I am feeling. While I need those people to help encourage me when I am mourning a loss, I don't want to be encouraged. I just want somebody to sit and cry with me, be angry for me, and validate that what I am feeling is real. I already know that I can't stay feeling this way, and most of the time, I likely already know all the good things in my life. This is not about dismissing those things. This is about feeling the loss and mourning it. There are some people in your life who are just better at this than others. And to be fair, you may need to announce ahead of time that you are just wanting to mourn a loss.

My wife is a constant encourager. She can be very bubbly. While this has been extremely helpful in allowing me to get out of some funks I get in from time to time, when I am just sad and want to mourn a loss, it can be very annoying. On the flip side, when she just wants to be encouraged when she is sharing something that is keeping her down and I sit shiva with her, it is not what she needs. I mention this, particularly for couples going through this journey, as your spouse may not be the best or only person you need to mourn something with. And if you are going to process things with them, give them a heads-up before you start. You and your spouse may be mourning the same loss, but you are likely not mourning it in the same way or on the same timeline. It can be easy for this to lead to conflict. Not that you are against each other; it is just that you are in different stages of grief.

While you might process some things internally and release them, I have noticed with grief it can build up. At some point, you may need more than just you to talk to. You might need to do this out loud with somebody.

When you have taken time to name the loss, you have spoken it out loud to somebody, the next step is to release it. You can release it in a few different ways. Just speaking it can be a release for some. For others, you may need to bury it. By bury it, I mean dig an actual hole and put something in the hole that represents the loss, then fill the hole in. Maybe you write it down and burn it in a fire. Put it on a stone and throw it into a lake. Write it on a bottle of Tannerite and blow it up. Whatever and however works for you, the point is you need something to help remind you that you have released it. The reminder is an important part of the healing journey. When future you is tempted to yearn for it, remembering that you released it will allow you to continue forward.

The comparison trap can easily ensnare you into trying to adopt somebody else's purpose and goals as your own. It is good to have inspiration from others, but they do not have your child, your resources, and your situation. For your purpose and your goals for parenting, they need to be just that…yours. What works for others is great for them, but you need to find what works for you.

I wish I had a nice little four-step plan on how to find your purpose. As much as I would want to make this neat and easy, my biggest encouragement to you as you continue down this journey is to get as healthy as you possibly can; healthy physically, healthy financially, healthy emotionally, healthy relationally, and healthy spiritually. As you prioritize your own personal health, you will see your situation through a different lens. This may require you to get some respite care. Allowing somebody else to step in and provide some relief for you so you can take some time to work on yourself is perfectly okay to do. In fact, this may be the best thing you will ever do for your person. By taking the time to be a better you, you can then be a better caregiver. Remember, this entire section is asking, "Is it me?". While you are not causing autism, ADHD, adolescence, or even a-hole, you can certainly negatively impact all of this if you are not the best you. As you go down this journey of getting healthy, I don't expect some magically wonderful purpose to suddenly appear, but I have found that you are much more likely to find it when you are healthy than when you are not.

The more I am rested, living healthily, and living in community with others, the easier it is for me to recognize that I am a part of something bigger. Even the writing of this book is about telling my story, not so much that I have it all figured out, but that I am in the struggle every day and continuing to be in the struggle is part of my purpose. I hope this book encourages you to know you are not alone on the journey. And if you will allow yourself a chance to see it, there are others around you who are watching you do what you do. They do not know how you do it, and desperately want to help you, but just the fact that you keep doing it is inspiring to them. You are a bigger part of the story than you might think. Staying faithful to your journey has meaning.

Healthy people in your life, whether friends or professionals you have hired, will also be able to ask you questions and help pull out your purpose. You may have to let go of some older purposes you have lived by, and you may have to rediscover some old purposes you have walked away from.

But please hear this: IT IS WORTH IT! It is worth taking the time to find your purpose. It is worth the energy you put into it. It is worth it for you, it is worth it for your person, and it is worth it for society that you take the time to know why you are doing what you are doing.

Here are a few questions to help you pull out what your purpose might be. I am intentionally asking these questions from multiple angles. Some are from a positive perspective, others are from a negative perspective. You may find it difficult to identify the positive, but if you can easily see the negative, you can work backwards from there. As see these answers more clearly, hopefully you can find the pieces to developing a purpose. So here goes:

1. What aspect of parenting brings you the most fulfillment?

2. What are you doing as a parent when you feel the most failure?

3. When have you felt like you were really winning as a parent?

4. What causes you to want to give up?

5. What is the most encouraging thing that somebody can do for you?

6. What is the most discouraging thing somebody has done to you?

7. What do you see in others that causes you the most envy?

8. How confident are you in your child's abilities? Do you know what they are realistically capable of accomplishing in life? If not, is there somebody you might speak to about this? Like a teacher or one of your child's professionals? Knowing what your child is capable of can help further define purpose.

9. What has your child voiced as what they want for themselves?

10. What purpose did your parents have for you?

11. If you fulfilled your purpose, how would you know it?

A New Kind of SMART

A purpose needs to be enacted. Having a purpose is great, but if you don't have any way to put it into practice, it is like having a car with no fuel for the engine. It looks really cool, but it will go nowhere. One way we can help engage and measure progress of a purpose is through goals.

These goals may not mean much to others, but that is okay because your goals are not their goals. What is right for you may not be right for them. Setting Specific, Measurable, Achievable, Realistic, and Time-bound (SMART) goals is the normal advice for goal setting, but I have learned that with parenting someone with specialized needs, those specific goals need to be flexible. You can't always measure measurable goals objectively; sometimes they need to be felt. What is achievable and realistic can sometimes track, but often needs to be adjusted along the way. And seldom do any of these things occur within the initially planned timeframe. This may sound like I am speaking out of both sides of my mouth by saying to set goals, but I want to encourage you to allow the goals you set to have the ability to be changed and adjusted. Let me see if I can make sense of it. If you can set and achieve traditional SMART goals, great! Set those goals and rock on. But I have found in my life that I needed to give my SMART goals some grace.

As we talk about purpose, the purpose will probably not change, but the goals you use to accomplish that purpose might need to. For instance, my son received an early diagnosis, so my wife and I quickly agreed on the purpose of helping him achieve maximum independence and function at his highest capacity. However, as much as this was our purpose, we had, and still do not have, any idea of what his ultimate limits are. Some of his early milestones for development he hit, but he hit them significantly behind his peers. But he still hit them. I'm referring to milestones such as walking, speaking, reading, and jumping (which took some time). Some of these involved natural development, while others related to cognitive abilities or disabilities. So while our purpose did not change, our goals needed to be flexible in order to accommodate his developmental ability.

Measurement is a good thing in goal setting. And typically you want those measurements to be objective and easily observable by others. And if you can find measurable goals, great, but sometimes some goals resist objective measurement. My wife and I found that some of our measurements were internal. When he started to walk, sure, we could measure the steps, and as he started to read, we could count the words and measure the comprehension levels based on difficulty of the material and reading comprehension quizzes, but there were other parts of those goals that had to be felt. Were we doing the best we could to help him accomplish the purpose of being independent? We were super excited as his ability to read grew, but as it related to our purpose, were we doing what we could to help grow this into independence? In order for us to know we were accomplishing the purpose, we needed to feel the measurement, not just observe it. And please hear me, it is easy to skip this step. It is easy to just check the box and not feel it, but it is important to take the time to celebrate the feeling behind it. As you reinforce the meaning of the measurement, it will help you stay on purpose.

There is no handbook for parenting a special needs child. This is part of the reason that I wrote this. Not that this is going to address all issues with special needs parenting, but I had little to go on when we went through this. The adage of building the plane while you are flying it seems very true with special needs parenting. If you have picked this up while you are on your journey, I hope and pray that it is a valuable resource for you. A resource that I could not easily find on my journey.

Because there is not a handbook, finding objective measures to guide you can be scarce. And that is okay. Your purpose for your child may not be all that easily measured. But it is possible to feel it. Please know I am not discounting measuring progress, but I am for including the intangibles into the measurement process. Especially when those intangibles are all you have some days. Knowing that you are on your path, even when others can't observe it, is a huge measurement to acknowledge.

Achievable and realistic are still part of the equation, but they may have to be adjusted along the way. To stick with reading, even as he began to read, we needed to recognize that just because he could recognize and pronounce the words, his ability to comprehend what they were saying was limited. It was and is great that he could read them, but as the purpose was independence, what was achievable with reading needed to be adjusted to focus more on the comprehension piece. And while it would be great if he could read literary classics and write papers on them, he needs to read instruction manuals and follow the directions; read road signs and maps to know where to go. Read a menu and tell somebody what he wants. These are all tenets of independence. And to be perfectly honest, in first or second grade, we had hopes this would be realistic and achievable, but we did not know how much he would be able to accomplish this, given his limitations.

Time-bound is one of my larger frustrations with this process. There is SO MUCH waiting. Not just the annoying waiting at a red light, but waiting to see how much he will develop and accomplish. Will he reach a plateau? How will we know when he does? Will he regress once he reaches a plateau? Because we kept sensing that he had not reached his limit, we kept pushing. And sometimes, the pace has seemed incredibly slow. But we have had to keep pushing. Other times, when we have seen regression, we have had to stop and evaluate what might be contributing. Sometimes, we have found out about bullies that have set him back; other times we have concluded that medications (sometimes the absence of medications, other times negative impacts of present medications) have contributed to these regressions. But we have to keep pushing.

As you are developing your purpose, and please hear me that the purpose for my kid will not be the same as your purpose for your kid, you must have a purpose you can keep pushing for. Because the goals are going to be a different kind of SMART: Stretchable, Meaningful, Adjustable, Realistic, Time-Framed.

Specificity is excellent, but you will inevitably fail if it is so precise that it cannot accommodate shifting situations. I heard an old missionary say once, "blessed are the flexible for they shall not break". This has been a foundation in my journey as a special needs parent. Try to make a goal as specific as possible, but make sure it has room to stretch when circumstances change; when the toy gets lost, the meds have a negative reaction, or it is just overstimulating.

Measurement is necessary, but make sure you are measuring everything: the observable and the intangible. Having this measurement be meaningful to you personally and to your overall purpose will be a better sign of whether your goals are on point with your purpose.

What is attainable sometimes has to be adjusted. Sometimes this is a day-to-day adjustment, sometimes this is an overall course redirection. Adjusting a goal is not a failure but a better understanding of the reality of your situation. You are still on purpose, but you may just have to adjust how you get there.

Please set goals to enact your purpose, but be SMART about it, and if necessary, the new kind of SMART.

Maybe It's Not About You

What I am about to say, I don't like that I am saying it. I don't like it, but I recognize it is true. Sometimes the purpose for why you do what you do might not be about you. Your continuing on the journey might positively impact somebody else. You doing what you do can be a great encouragement to others, a significant challenge to others, and may even be an inspiration to others. While it may not help you in your situation (which is why I don't enjoy talking about this), sometimes it is not about me. Sometimes, I have a job to do, and doing it is not so much for my benefit but for the benefit of others. However, people can certainly overdo this (codependency comes to mind), but I must believe a bigger story is unfolding, and completing that larger mission might not always be the easiest or most considerate choice for me, but somewhere and somehow, and for somebody, it has value.

The more isolated you are, the less likely you are to see this. Being in community with others (even if that community might not fully get your situation or have nothing obvious to offer you in your situation) is a way to tell your story. Your story may be the inspiration others need to enact change. While it might not change things for you, it might impact how another person interacts with a special needs family in public. It could change how someone invests their time and resources to volunteer to help. It may also change how they vote or whether they run for political office.

Many of the help and resources my family is a beneficiary of is because somebody else was inspired to take action. Special Olympics is not something I started, but somebody else's journey. Her sister, Rosemary, inspired Eunice Kennedy Shriver, the founder of Special Olympics, and that inspiration led to a worldwide organization. I greatly benefit from this organization that was inspired by others. Many of the benefits of the Americans with Disabilities Act that my person takes advantage of came to be because others stood up and spoke about their experiences and inspired change.

While it may not be a game-changer for now, living out and telling your story has a purpose. If you do not share your story with others, you limit the impact your person can have on society. It is okay to share your struggles and successes with others. You don't want to be the consistently negative person, but being able to share your struggles helps others understand as best as they can the situation you are in. But don't just share your struggles. Share when you meet a goal, or an unexpected blessing comes your way. Surround yourself with a cheering squad that celebrates your successes and offers comfort during your failures. Living out your story so that others can see it opens up possibilities not just for support in the now, but for change in the future.

Here are a few questions as you consider how you and your story might impact others.

1. What is the best way for you to communicate with others? (Phone call, meet up, text message, social media, etc.)

2. When something great happens, who do you call? (And if you just said Ghostbusters, we can be friends!)

3. When you need to vent, who do you tell?

4. Are these the same people? If not, why?

5. Who speaks life into you?

6. Who genuinely wants to know how things are going?

7. Who does your person want to be around?

8. How are you telling your story?

9. Is it easier to share successes or struggles? Why?

10. Whose story do you most want to hear?

Gratitude

Did you read the title of this section and are having trouble deciding whether you want to read it? Me too. I am having difficulty writing it. The deeper you get into the struggle of special needs parenting, those burdens you carry around on the regular are not exactly something you want to include on your Christmas brag letter. (You know, the letter you include with your Christmas card to tell how great things are.)

When we talk about gratitude, I am not talking about trying to gaslight yourself into believing that all these really terrible things that are happening to you are good. "I am so thankful I got cussed out and attacked last night by my child!" But I am talking about finding things within the struggle to be grateful for and taking time to express that.

In my years as a therapist, I have found that (and there are exceptions here) depressed people are rarely grateful, and grateful people are rarely depressed. Taking the time to acknowledge the good in your life, and then taking the next step to act on that acknowledgment and express it, changes something about you. This really is a skill you can develop. And this can also be contagious.

For example, if you are alive and breathing, you have something to be thankful for. You are reading this book, so you can see and read. If somebody is reading it to you, you can hear. For those of us in this exclusive club that nobody wanted to join, being a parent/guardian of someone with special needs has taught you to look at the good in situations, so you can celebrate the smallest of victories. For example, a few weeks ago, my person got very angry and knocked a hole in the wall. The way it was told to me was that he threw his flip-flop at the wall and knocked a hole in the drywall. While I was angry and upset, I remember telling my wife that he was able to achieve an impressive amount of velocity in that throw if he knocked a hole that big with a flip-flop! (Come to find out, he kicked the hole in the wall while wearing his flip-flops, but the point remains: even in a bad situation I was looking for something to celebrate!)

I need to hold myself accountable regarding one aspect of gratitude. This is something I do, and think I am experiencing gratitude, but I am going to call BS on myself, and you too if you do this. I have frequently tried to rationalize my experience by trying to convince myself that somehow this journey that I am on with my child could be way worse. And somehow, the struggles he has have prevented him from being in a way worse situation. Meaning, this chaotic journey I am on is some sort of kindness because if he did not have these struggles, perhaps he would be in a horrific situation. I tell myself things like, had he not faced these struggles, a terror group might have radicalized him into committing terrible violence against innocent people. Therefore, I should be thankful that God may have permitted him to have these struggles to avert a dreadful future he could be enduring. Maybe God allowed him in my life to humble and grow me, and keep me from being a truly terrible person.

While these could be true, saying these things and calling it gratitude is cheating. Instead of being grateful for what I am not, I need to be grateful for what I am. For example, it is perfectly good to be grateful for the things you have learned on the journey. I can and need to be grateful for the insights I discovered, for the patience I learned, and for the empathy I developed. Those are great things to be grateful for, and I need to express that. But I don't need to be grateful for not being an a-hole! (Partly because I am an a-hole, just ask my wife!!)

In scripture, in Luke 18, verses 9-14, Jesus tells us a contrast of two men going to the temple to pray. One, a religious leader whom society, and himself, considered better than everybody else; better spiritually and better financially. His prayer was, "God, I thank you that I am not like other people—robbers, evildoers, adulterers—or even like this tax collector."[1] The other person, you guessed it, was the tax collector, the person whom society, and himself, considered as being less than everybody else. His prayer was, "God, have mercy on me, a sinner."[2] Jesus had praise for the humble man, but condemnation for the arrogant one.

As I focus on all the things I am not, even the horrible things I could be, I am exercising pride. I know, this sounds messed up, but even in my horrible situation when I am comparing myself to those worse than me and am grateful that "I am not like this other man…" I am just as proud and arrogant as the Pharisee in the book of Luke. But when I focus on my situation and take stock of the blessings that God has given me, I am humble and much more pleasant to be around. I am a better person when I am thankful for what I have than when I am thankful for what I don't have.

Gratitude is more than just acknowledging the good in your life; it has a necessary and valuable second part. You have read it a few times already in this section, but I want to take a minute to call it out specifically and discuss it. You have to express your gratitude. Acknowledging it internally is great, but to get the full impact of it, you need to express it. This could be a prayer to God expressing your gratitude. This is not bad, but there are times and even seasons when it is really hard to do this. I have also found that there is a certain power in expressing this to others. Telling someone else how you are

---

[1] Luke 18:11 NIV
[2] Luke 18:13 NIV

genuinely thankful for something in your life is like the difference between scare power and laugh power in Monsters Inc. If you are not familiar with the reference, in the movie (spoiler alert) when they get kids to laugh, this is exponentially more powerful than when they get kids to scream out of fear. Sure, screams (complaining) generate some power, but laughs (gratefulness) blew circuits because they collected so much power.

Please hear me; there is value in being able to vent to others. We have gone over that previously. That needs to happen. But for true health to occur, you need to express your gratitude as well. I apologize in advance for the graphic nature of this example, but vents are like vomiting. Sometimes you need to get the poison out. Your body knows there is poison in your stomach and it needs to vomit to get rid of it. Venting is like your brain vomiting. Keeping it in will destroy you. Gratitude is like eating healthy food, taking vitamins, and exercising. It may not get the immediate feeling of relief that vomiting can bring, but it is bringing life and health to you. It is protecting you from diseases by boosting your immune system and keeping you out of unhealthy situations. I am not telling you not to vent, but I am encouraging you to make a point to express gratitude to others. I would challenge you with this. The more you express gratitude to others, the less you will need to vent to them. Once again, venting is not bad, but by the time you get to venting, things have already built up to an unhealthy point. I would much rather you process your situation with gratitude rather than wait until it builds up and have to vent it.

If you don't have people in your life at this point to express gratitude to, I would encourage (even if you have people, this encouragement still stands) to write down the things you have to be grateful for. Get a journal or a notes app and just write down the things you have to be thankful for. Keep a running list. Write it down and date it. There are a few ways this has the potential to be helpful. One, it lets you express your gratitude. Two, when the time comes where you have difficulties finding things to be grateful for, you can read this list. You can be an encouragement to future you by taking the time to express your gratitude.

Gratitude Prompts:

1. What is something good that happened to you today?

2. What good thing do you have in your life that you do not deserve?

3. In what way was someone kind to you today?

4. What were you able to give to someone else today?

5. What is working like it should right now?

6. What basic needs are currently met?

7. If your home were on fire, what would you take with you? (Be thankful for whatever you would take with you)

8. What have you accomplished today? (Think small: this could be getting out of bed or peeing in the toilet versus on yourself. You don't have to cure cancer here!)

9. What challenge did you overcome today?

10. How have you expressed your gratitude today?

Final Thoughts

My hope, goal, and prayer is that this has helped you better evaluate the sources of behaviors in your person, and helped you look within yourself to make sure you are as healthy as you can be, because this journey into special needs parenting will require the best of you. The specialized needs of autism, ADHD, and adolescence are a challenge. Each one individually is a challenge, but add them all together and put in a touch of a-hole, and it can be overwhelming. I hope this has provided you with a new set of glasses through which to evaluate your situation differently. I sincerely hope you take the time to check your own health as well. This process can be draining, and if you are feeling alone on this journey, please know that you are not.

For those who are reading this book and are not experiencing this journey directly, but are here trying to better understand a friend or family member's situation, I want to extend my gratitude to you. While reading this book will not make you immediately qualified to diagnose or "fix" anyone in your life, I do hope it will help you listen better, ask questions better, cry with them better, celebrate better, and just be a better source of hope, help, and health. If after reading this you still have questions, GREAT! Find healthy ways to ask your friend or family member. As one who is on this journey, I can tell you I am not upset when someone asks me a question, even if it is a stupid question, but is asking it because they love and are concerned. What I get frustrated with is questions that are asked out of judgement and condemnation. And if you ask a question, stick around for the answer. You may not like it. And sometimes, the answers that you get might need to be challenged. You are in a unique situation (being outside of the experience) to challenge a thought or provide a different perspective. Nobody likes a know-it-all, but healthy people will welcome somebody to challenge them lovingly.

For those on the journey, share your experiences. Nobody will know what you are going through unless you tell them. Who knows what type of help the group you are in may have, and you will never know unless you voice your need and share your story. And if you had to discover or fabricate your own resources along the way, please share them with others. Share on social media, start a podcast, write a book, or find new ways to share. We are not on this journey alone, and we need to hear from each other.